THE WELSH REVIVAL

THE WELSH REVIVAL

Its Origin and Development

THOMAS PHILLIPS

THE BANNER OF TRUTH TRUST

THE BANNER OF TRUTH TRUST
3 Murrayfield Road, Edinburgh EH12 6EL
PO Box 621, Carlisle, Pennsylvania 17013, USA

*

© *The Banner of Truth Trust 1989*
First published 1860
First Banner of Truth edition 1989
Reprinted 1995
Reprinted 1998
Reprinted 2002
ISBN 0 85151 685 8

*

Printed and bound in Finland by
WS Bookwell

PREFACE.

THE writer of the following pages, while sympathising most heartily with the revival in Wales, feels some difficulty in becoming its historian. He must confess that, since the meeting in the Mansion House in November last, when the revival in Ireland was made the leading topic, both in the addresses and the prayers, he has often thought and said, "Oh that some one would tell the story of the Welsh revival to these and other dear Christian friends!" Soon after this, he was asked by his esteemed friend and neighbour, the Rev. John Venn of Hereford, to give his people an "Address on the Revival in Wales"—a request with which he gladly complied, and many of the facts given in the present publication were related on that occasion.

Again and again he has been urged, by many highly valued friends, both in England and Wales, to give a sketch of this remarkable religious movement. He pleaded constant occupation in the service of one of the leading public societies, as a reason why he should decline the task. At the same time, he felt the force of the remarks made by many friends—" You have travelled the length and breadth of the land; you know and speak the language of the people; you are, from your office, necessarily acquainted with the leading ministers and members of the various sections of the Christian Church in Wales; you have recently visited the scenes of the revival, and therefore you are well qualified to give us some account of it." All this may be very true; and as the writer cannot say that he is required to make " brick" without " straw," he has at length resolved to do what lay in his power to meet the wishes thus expressed.

In addition to all that he has seen and heard, he has in his possession a considerable number of letters and documents bearing on the awakening in Wales. But as most of these were originally written in the Welsh language, a free translation of their contents is here given. Some extracts have also been inserted from a pamphlet recently published, on the same subject, by the Rev. E. Davies, to whom the writer here expresses his obligation.

The difficulty has been to select and abridge, and so to arrange the materials as to avoid sameness and repetition on the one hand, and incompleteness on the other. It has been his aim to furnish a correct and impartial view, totally unfettered by any sectarian bias; and although he does not commit himself to an approval of all the external circumstances of this movement, whether in connexion with individuals or communities, he has no hesitation in saying, " This is the finger of God."

HEREFORD, *March* 24, 1860.

INTRODUCTION.

WHAT is there in this world of any real importance, or even of any real interest, compared with the progress of Christ's kingdom? Whenever one single individual is added to the number of Christ's followers, though he be one of the poorest and most despised of men, yet is his conversion the occasion of joy throughout heaven. "There is joy in the presence of the angels of God over one sinner that repenteth," was the solemn and emphatic declaration which our blessed Saviour twice uttered, and which He illustrated by three different parables. And need we wonder at this? When a sinner is converted, he is washed from all his sins in the blood of God's own incarnate Son; he is renewed after the Divine image, and made a temple of the Holy Ghost; he is saved from everlasting destruction, and invested with a title to eternal life; he is now a king and a priest with God; and he will one day be made perfect in holiness, and have his vile body fashioned like unto Christ's glorious body, and shine like the sun in his Father's kingdom, and through all eternity shew forth the praises of his God and Saviour—a monument of infinite power, and wisdom, and grace, and love.

Nearly six thousand years have now passed since sin entered into the world, and death by sin ; and though, during that period, the Holy Spirit has been continually putting forth His power in the conversion of sinners, and an innumerable company has been gathered into the kingdom of heaven, yet how wide has the dominion of Satan ever been, and how few and partial have been the seasons of " revival ! "

But, thank God, the days in which we now live are days of blessedness and glory ! The kingdom of Christ is now everywhere making unexampled progress. Sinners are being brought to repentance, not in small numbers—" one of a city, and two of a family," (or tribe)—but in multitudes !

It may be too much, perhaps, to affirm that, for the last year or two, every day has been, as regards the number converted, *a day of Pentecost.* But yet, in the North of Ireland alone, it has been calculated that at one time one thousand sinners were being daily awakened to a serious concern about their souls ; whilst God was carrying on His work in Wales, and Sweden, and America, with almost equal rapidity ; and in other parts of the world, such as England, Scotland, Africa, India, &c., with a far more than ordinary rapidity. So that we shall not, perhaps, greatly err, if we suppose that a total number of nearly three thousand souls has, on an average, during the last year or two, been daily added to the Church of Christ.

We have, however, not only cause to rejoice when we consider the vast multitudes of sinners that have been so lately translated out of darkness into the kingdom of God's dear Son; we may also rejoice, when we think of the way in which He has been pleased to revive His work, at the same time, among His own people. He who has quickened so many that were dead in trespasses and sins, has also visited His Church, and filled the hearts of numbers with the spirit of prayer, and of love to the brethren, and of compassion for perishing sinners. The very sight of such multitudes, suddenly quickened into life by God's sovereign and mighty power, and brought, through overwhelming convictions of sin, into a state of peace and joy unspeakable, and then filled with burning zeal, has been like new life to the Church itself.

What is the state of things which may soon—even before this generation has passed away—be witnessed? The whole heathen world is being rapidly opened to the gospel. The two great powers that have for ages opposed its progress throughout a large portion of the earth—Popery and Mohammedanism—are giving daily proofs of weakness and decay. In Protestant countries God is reviving His work, and is raising up a missionary army, composed of the true soldiers of the Cross, to take the field under Christ their great Captain. Are we on the eve of the fulfilment of that great prophecy?—" Every valley shall be exalted, and every mountain and hill shall be made low; and the crooked shall be made straight, and the rough places plain: and the glory of the Lord shall be revealed, and all flesh shall see it together; for the mouth of the Lord hath spoken it."

Little, comparatively, has been known in England, of the revival in Wales. The difference of language has proved a great barrier against the investigation of the work by English Christians; and yet the character of this revival is deeply interesting, and its results have already been most marvellous. It may well be doubted whether anything has taken place in Ireland, or in America, or in any part of the world, since the Day of Pentecost, more truly wonderful than the revival at Festiniog, as described in the following pages.

Hitherto, no account appears to have been published, that has taken a *comprehensive* view of the revival in Wales. The account now brought before the public is necessarily, indeed, a mere outline of what God is doing; but it gives a comprehensive view of the work as it is going on throughout the principality, and in connexion with all denominations of Christians. I may be permitted to add, that all who have the pleasure and the privilege of knowing its author, are well aware that no one could have been found better qualified for the task. He undertook it in compliance with the earnest solicitations of his friends, and he has now faithfully executed it, though in the midst of overwhelming labours, in the cause to which he has for so many years, and with such zeal and ability, devoted himself —the cause of the British and Foreign Bible Society.

May the reading of this little publication be abundantly blessed to many! And whilst it awakens emotions of wonder, and thankfulness, and joy, in the hearts of God's people, may it encourage them to pray yet more earnestly, and with a more lively faith and hope, for a similar revival in England!

J. VENN.

HEREFORD, *March* 21, 1860.

CONTENTS.

PRELIMINARY OBSERVATIONS.

CHAPTER I.

ORIGIN, PROGRESS, AND EXTENT.

CHAPTER II.

SCENES OF REVIVAL—SOUTH WALES.

CHAPTER III.

SCENES OF REVIVAL—NORTH WALES.

CHAPTER IV.

RESULTS.

CHAPTER V.

GENERAL EFFECTS.

CHAPTER VI.

PRINCIPAL FEATURES.

CHAPTER VII.

CONCLUDING REMARKS.

- - -

APPENDIX.

THE WELSH REVIVAL.

PRELIMINARY OBSERVATIONS.

WHAT eventful days are these in which we live! How full of action! Nothing seems to be at rest. Whether we turn our eyes to the political, or the scientific, or the intellectual, or the religious world, there is everywhere an uneasy travailing, a spirit of unrest, to be seen. The work of a century is crowded into a year. If important events had succeeded each other as rapidly from the beginning of the world as they do now, any tolerably full knowledge of history would be an impossible acquirement. But it may be that the time is short, and that there are yet many things remaining to be accomplished. Who can foresee what may be the condition of the nations of Europe even in one short year? Will it be peace? The Lord only knows. He works out His own purposes in His own way, and by His own instruments. But we will not fear, come what may— "He doeth all things well;" and if we love Him, we may be sure that all things, whether in the great world or in our own more immediate circle, will "work together for our good."

But while the principles of evil and selfishness in a variety of forms are more active now than at any former period in the world's history, it is very gratifying to see that God has at the same time put it into the heart of His own people to be more zealous and active in their efforts to extend His kingdom. Every new discovery in science is pressed into this service. The DIVINE WORD, translated into nearly all languages, is now multiplied to an unprecedented extent, and with incredible rapidity circulated throughout the habitable globe. Nor do the preachers and teachers of that WORD lag behind, for there never was a time in which so many earnest men presented themselves to the different missionary societies and asked to be "sent" in obedience to the Divine command, "Go ye into all the world, and preach the gospel to every creature."

But the best feature of all in the aspect of the present times, and the most cheering and grateful to the mind of all God's children, is the fact, now acknowledged even by the world, that there is a power at work in the hearts and consciences of people not to be accounted for by any human hypothesis. Attempts have been made to explain the cause of the wonderful phenomena which have been observed in this and in other countries accompanying the feeling of deep conviction of sin, but all confessedly equally unsatisfactory.

And all other explanations than the true one must necessarily be so. This, however, is a very simple one, though it may require Faith to receive and adopt it—these are "times of refreshing from the PRESENCE OF THE LORD."

The Lord has caused His people to feel more deeply than ever the need of a gracious REVIVAL, not only in the world, but also in the Church; and this feeling has found expression in prayer, more generally and more intensely than at any former period within our memory. In the closet, at the family altar, and in the public congregation, this great blessing has been sought with persevering earnestness. Even in prayer it has been found that "union is strength." In numerous instances Christian congregations, in addition to the usual or special gathering for prayer in their own sanctuaries, have united with others for this high and holy purpose in some public room, or alternately in their several places of worship. Meetings for prayer have been held in all sorts of places, and attended by all sorts of people. In churches and chapels, in vestries and school-rooms, in town-halls and market-places, in the covered tent and in the open field, in the recesses of the forest and on the mountain top, in the saloons of steamers, and on the open decks of sailing vessels—meetings for special prayer have been held; and in some instances, elegant drawing-rooms have been thrown open for this purpose, while, on a late memorable occasion, the Egyptian Hall of the Mansion House was converted for the time into a Christian oratory. In all these places, from the lips and hearts of the thousands who attended them, ONE PRAYER has ascended up before God's throne: "O Lord, revive Thy work in the midst of the years"—"Wilt Thou not revive us again, that Thy people may rejoice in Thee?" And the blessing thus ardently and generally sought, has been graciously vouchsafed. Verily there is a God who hears and answers prayer. The Christian Church has been greatly revived in this and in other lands. While the kingdom of darkness has been sensibly shaken, multitudes have been made to feel that religion is indeed a reality. The Revival, so called, is one of the great topics of the day. No section of the community is able to ignore it. The pulpit, the platform, and the press all unite to proclaim the wonderful religious movement of the times in which we live.

AMERICA was the first to wake up from her awful spiritual torpor; and it is said that no fewer than six hundred thousand persons in the United States have, within the last two years, been led to make a profession of religion.

ENGLAND has not been wholly forgotten; for although we cannot yet speak of any great and overwhelming movement in any one locality, yet in many places, both in the metropolis and elsewhere, "the Spirit of God is moving upon the face of the waters," and now and again makes His presence felt, by mighty operations upon the hearts and consciences of sinners.

SCOTLAND has been visited with a gracious shower, as the accounts from Glasgow, Edinburgh, Aberdeen, and many other places testify.

IRELAND also is now thoroughly awake, rising out of the dust, and putting on her beautiful garments.

SWEDEN likewise is experiencing a powerful and widespread revival, chiefly as the result of Scripture circulation, and the evangelistic efforts of those who have themselves known by experience the power of the truth.

And lastly, to return home, the principality of WALES, by no means a stranger to revivals * in years gone by, has

---

* It would be difficult to furnish the exact number and dates of the revivals with which the principality has been favoured. The first commenced at Llangeitho in 1739. The "great revival" as it is called, commenced in 1762. There was another in 1791, and a most remarkable awakening took place in 1817. Between these dates, there were revivals on a smaller scale, and since the latter date, there have been awakenings in different parts of Wales. During the revival of 1840, more than two thousand members were added to the Calvinistic Methodists alone, in the small county of Merioneth. Anglesea and Carnarvonshire were blessed with a powerful revival in 1848, and the following year. It is reported that one of the revivals at Llangeitho had its commencement in a feeling awakened in the minds of the people, while the Rev. Daniel

also in these days been blessed with an abundant outpouring of " the latter rain."

In the following pages, the revival in Wales will be regarded in its origin, progress, and extent, together with its results and principal features. And it is hoped that this brief view of the work of God's Holy Spirit in the principality—a work still going on, and still increasing and deepening—may fill the hearts of the reader with feelings of joy and gratitude, akin to those which animated the audience of Peter, when after hearing his narrative, they "glorified God, and said, Then hath God given to the Gentiles repentance unto life."

Rowland was reading the Litany—more especially the impressive words, " by thine agony and bloody sweat," &c. And another great revival followed the introduction of a volume of Welsh Hymns, composed by the Rev. William Williams of Pantycelyn.

CHAPTER I.

ORIGIN, PROGRESS, AND EXTENT.

It is difficult to trace the *origin* of some things which are now great and formidable : their beginning was small, and all the early circumstances are lost in doubt and uncertainty. We discover the origin of rivers by tracing them to their source. If we stand on the banks of the deep Severn at Gloucester, or the beautiful Wye at Hereford, or the wild and capricious Rheidol at Aberystwyth, and ask, Whence do these rivers come? we may be told, that if we follow those streams to their fountain-head, we shall find ourselves at length ascending the gentle declivities of Plinlimmon. There we shall find those small springs which, in their progress towards the ocean, gradually swell, and widen, and deepen, bestowing fertility and beauty upon large and extensive tracts of country. Not far from that mountain we shall find the localities where the first outbursts of thought and feeling were witnessed in fervent prayer, faithful preaching, and house to house exhortation ; and which like so many living streams now spread over the land, rising and swelling, widening and deepening, in their onward course, bringing with them abundance of revival blessings to many thousands of Welsh " hearts and homes."

Whatever awakenings of lesser extent may have been felt in some places previously, there can be no doubt that,

as far as *South Wales* is concerned, the present revival
commenced on, or near the banks of the Ystwyth in Cardiganshire. The places named as having first manifested a
more than ordinary concern for religion are, Tre'r-ddal,
Yspytty, Ystum-tyhen, Cwmystwyth, and some other localities in the same remote region. It is said that the work
commenced chiefly by the instrumentality of Humphrey
Jones and David Morgan, the former a preacher amongst
the Wesleyans, and the latter amongst the Calvinistic Methodists. Mr Jones had emigrated to the United States,
and having witnessed much of the revival work in that
country, he was now anxious on his return to his native place
to witness a similar outpouring of God's Holy Spirit there.
We are told that he addressed his discourses to professing
Christians, chiefly with a view to rouse them to greater life
and activity, maintaining, it is presumed, that an *awakened
church* is to be the principal instrument in converting the
world. It is said that the first intercourse between these
two men was most solemn. Being engaged in the same
work, they interchanged views and feelings very freely.
Mr Jones spoke to Mr Morgan very strongly on the state
of religion in the country ; the deadness of the churches,
and the necessity of more earnest prayer. The character
of the ministry was dwelt upon—that the gospel should be
preached with more directness and energy—to be followed
up by personal labours amongst the people.

"Mr Morgan was at first prejudiced against Mr Jones'
proceedings, but what he said to him had such a powerful
effect upon his mind, that he could get no sleep for several
nights, but continued in earnest prayer for the guidance of
the Spirit. Mr Morgan went again to see Mr Jones, and
said, 'We cannot do much harm by keeping prayer-meetings, and trying to rouse the country, even if there be

nothing but man in it after all.' 'You cannot do any harm,' Mr Jones replied; 'and if you try it, you will not be long before God will be with you.' The next Sabbath-day Mr Morgan heard Mr Jones preach from 'Woe to them that are at ease in Zion;' and this sermon took so strong a hold of Mr Morgan's mind, that he was at once aroused to the work. A person who was present at this service writes: 'There was no visible effect during the preaching of this sermon; and in the *society** afterwards, Mr Jones said he had found it very hard to preach. One of the elders got up and said it was a very difficult thing for a man to say 'Amen,' under a ministry which he felt condemning him; and as he said these words he sat down as if fainting away. At this moment, there was something (I cannot say what it was, but that it was *something* that neither I nor any one else present had ever felt before) went through the whole congregation, until every one put down his head and wept! The following week the two churches, Wesleyan and Calvinistic Methodists, united to

---

* The members meet apart from the rest of the congregation for the purpose of transacting church business, admitting new members, administering discipline, and making preparations for the monthly communion. When confined to this kind of work, the church-meetings are held once in the month. But more frequently such meetings are held weekly, and in addition to the transaction of church business, the greater part of the time is taken up with read-ing the Scriptures, praise, prayer, mutual exhortation, instruction of the young, &c., &c. They are sometimes called "*Society*" meet-ings, and sometimes, "*Experience*" meetings. Nor are these meet-ings confined wholly to the various nonconforming communities, for in many places, the evangelical clergy have meetings of the same kind amongst the communicants. It will be seen that during the present revival, it has been the custom to hold a second service after the sermon, those only remaining who were either members already, or desirous of becoming candidates for church-fellowship.

keep prayer-meetings every night alternately, and we soon had a proof that the Lord was willing to accept our offerings, for there was a sweet-smelling savour accompanying them. Old backsliders began to return. Men came in crowds from the mountains, and all the country round, to our meetings, until we were afraid the chapel would come down,—men who were never seen in any place of worship, except in church at a christening or a funeral, and who knew nothing of worshipping God !"

Mr Morgan was by this time full of the spirit of revival, and was fully occupied during the day as well as every evening, in holding prayer-meetings, and conversing with inquirers. He was sent for to all the churches round, and wherever he went the Spirit was poured out, and scores of people came forward to seek a place in the house of God.

As these two men were thus greatly honoured of God at the commencement of the revival work, it may be interesting to know " what manner of persons" they were, and what was the character of their preaching. The following extract from a letter, written by Mr Jones to a young minister, will convey his own views of the Christian ministry, and we have good reason to believe that both he and Mr Morgan furnished, at that time, a living example of the description which he gives of the conditions of success in the Lord's work :—

" Two things are necessary to be a successful preacher : first, *to pray much in secret*—to be there many times in the day, wrestling with God—to wrestle each time as if it were the last, and not to rise from your knees until you have a proof that the Lord has heard you. Ask the Lord in faith, and with great fervency, what to say to the people. Go straight from your closet to the pulpit each time, (like Moses from the mount to the camp,) then will the anointing follow your preaching, and every word you say will be received as from an angel of God. Another thing is, *to preach pointedly and rousingly*—aiming at the conscience each time—telling the people their sins to their faces — caring nothing for the good or bad opinion of men, but to keep 'a conscience void of offence toward God and toward men ;' and beware of displaying yourself in any of your sermons. I try to aim at two things in studying and preaching : one is, not to say anything to show off myself; another is, not to say anything to amuse the people. I would wish to preach each time as if I had to die in the pulpit when I had done preaching—as if I had to go direct from the pulpit to judgment. If we are not in this frame, we shall do very little good."

It has been found, on inquiry, that at different times, and in different places, both in North and South Wales, there had been indications of a gracious reviving, previous to the movement to which we are about to call special attention. Amongst many other places may be mentioned Llanfair-fechan, Aber, and Penmaen-mawr, in Carnarvonshire. A communication from thence states :—" The revival of these latter years commenced here ; for in the year 1858 about 280 persons were added to the two denominations in this neighbourhood. These, with very few exceptions, are still pillars in the house of God.

"The year 1859, also, was a precious year to us in this place. Scores have been added to us already, and every week there are some additions made to the churches."

Trevecca, in Brecknockshire, the scene of many glorious revivals in the " good old times" of Howell Harries and Lady Huntingdon, and still a " school of the prophets," was favoured with an awakening during the winter of 1857 ; and the record of that gracious visitation should be preserved for the encouragement of such as feel interested in maintaining a high degree of pious ardour in the minds of those who are training for the Christian ministry. The Rev. D. Charles, president of the College, gives us the following narrative :—

"We were favoured with the first droppings of the shower at the College at Trevecca. An unusual spirit had possessed the students and the little church at this place for some time. You know that we are accustomed to hold weekly church-meetings in Wales, at which members relate the different dealings of God with their souls, when exhortations, warnings, and directions are given, suitable to the occasion, and the great truths of revelation are treated in their relation to living faith and practice. These our church-meetings had become as little Bethels to us for some months. The testimony of our consciences after each successive meeting was that God was there. We drank of that ' river the streams whereof make glad the city of God,' and were abundantly refreshed. We seemed at times to have arrived at the vestibule of heaven, where we could breathe its pure atmosphere, and join in the song of the redeemed in glory. One of these seasons of refreshing I shall never forget. The following is the account given by one of the young men present :—

" 'It has recently been our good fortune to be favoured with occasions of spiritual delight and blessing, and we cannot do other than rejoice at recalling and relating such glorious circumstances, which have been, in truth, a refreshing to our souls, and have awakened us, in some measure, from our stoical indifference to a greater earnestness in our own spiritual career, and also in that of others.

" 'The occasion on which the extraordinary manifestation of Divine favour referred to took place, was a church-meeting. As usual, two or three spoke their experience, and they did so with some feeling and unction. Thus the service was passing off pleasantly, every one feeling that it was good to be there. So far, however, there was nothing but what we had joyfully experienced many a time before. Still we were rejoiced, and felt inclined to thank God He had not forgotten us, and to pray that He would give yet more abundant proofs of His presence. But no one expected anything like so peculiar a manifestation as followed. Indeed, we could scarcely have formed any idea of such a manifestation, for the majority present had never seen anything like it. We had all heard our fathers speak of the great effects which they in their youth had seen accompanying the preaching of the word, and the influence which the outpouring of the Spirit was wont to have on the minds of the people assembled for worship ; but we had never seen the like ourselves, at least in the measure which our fathers were accustomed to say they had seen ; and, therefore, a kind of scepticism concerning its reality frequently possessed us. But now this scepticism was to be taken away for ever.

" ' Before separating, our beloved minister administered the sacrament of the Lord's Supper—peculiar circumstances rendering it necessary that this should be done in our church-meetings. And in reading the Word of God, and making a few passing remarks thereon, an influence was felt by all present, which we had never experienced in the like manner before. There was a beauty, a loveliness about the Holy Word which we had never hitherto perceived. New light seemed to be thrown upon it. It electrified us, and caused us to weep with joy. The feeling became general. All present were under its influence. The hardest hearts were forced to succumb. After some time we partook of the ordinance of the Lord's Supper, but under strange emotions. And then we sang, ay, sang with spirit, and repeated the hymn again and again—we could not leave off. Every heart seemed inspired to continue, and the last two lines were sung for full a quarter of an hour. Then the minister prayed, and such a prayer we had never before heard uttered. We felt that we were communing with God. Our hearts were truly poured out in praises and supplications. We could have prayed all night. But at length the prayer terminated, and we were to separate. But did we separate? Ah, no, every one resumed his seat and kept silence; and there we were for a length of time under the most heavenly feelings. Every heart was subdued. No one dared to speak, except by tears; and we were afraid lest any one should speak and put an end to the spell. We were at a loss to know what course should be adopted. Our feelings having been raised to so high a pitch, the difficulty was how to bring the service to a close, and to secure a separation without having the Divine influence marred. We were anxious that our impressions should continue. At length the minister rose, and slowly and pathetically read several appropriate portions of the Word of God. We then sang, and afterwards prayed again. And thus the meeting was carried on for four hours.

"'The effects were not transient. They have left a deep impression on our minds, and have influenced our conduct for good. We feel more serious, more ready to speak about our religious life, more anxious as regards the salvation of the world, and more desirous that the Lord would dwell amongst us, and favour us with a still greater outpouring of His holy Spirit. In truth "it was good to be there."'

"After the meeting I sat down with the young men, when each seemed to pour forth his whole heart into the bosom of his brother; and such was the Divine influence felt, that the place seemed to be filled with the special presence of God, which gave rise to the suggestion in my mind, 'Something like this must Pentecost have been.' 'How dreadful is this place! this is none other but the house of God, and this is the gate of heaven.' We were favoured after this with several meetings of a similar character, which have left very wholesome and valuable impressions upon the inmates of this institution."

Similar causes produced similar effects, and the revival made rapid *progress*. Other ministers entered the great field, baptized with the same spirit of earnestness and zeal for the Master's glory, and the salvation of souls. The "spirit of grace and supplications" was given to the churches, a revival in itself, and the means of procuring still greater blessings. The awakening influences at length reached the towns of Aberystwyth, Aberayron, Tregaron, and almost every district in the upper and middle parts of Cardiganshire. The celebrated Llangeitho, the ancient Zion, the scene of Daniel Rowland's devoted labours for more than forty years, was also visited with that revival power which on many former occasions had distinguished the place. The lower portions of the county, containing large and influential congregations, were also roused, and scenes of extraordinary interest were witnessed in many places. The fire was kindled, and the flame burst forth in the adjacent counties. In Merionethshire there is a glorious work in progress. Bala, so long honoured and blest by the labours of the apostolic Charles, is the scene of a powerful revival. At Dolgelly, and throughout the whole country lying between the rivers Dovey and Mowddy; from

Barmouth, along the sea-coast till we come to Harlech and Talsarnau ;—from thence to Maentwrog, Festiniog, and the quarry regions beyond, the mighty movement is felt. The counties of Carmarthen, Pembroke, Glamorgan, Brecknock, Radnor, and the Welsh parts of Monmouth, though not so deeply and thoroughly roused, have not been left unvisited. A prayerful spirit is general, and conversions in some places are very numerous. Indeed, in some districts of the counties here enumerated there are awakenings as powerful and as productive of good as we find in the most highly favoured districts. The same description applies to Montgomeryshire. Large portions of Flintshire and Denbighshire are stirred to their depth, and every week brings interesting reports of fresh movements in other towns and villages. Glorious tidings reach us from Carnarvonshire. The towns of Carnarvon, Bangor, Pwllhely, Portmadoc, Tremadoc, Conway, and Llandudno, are awakened to a blessed extent. The chief work, however, is in the vast slate-quarries, amongst the thousands who toil in the great excavations and caverns made by their own hard hands and strong arms. From Bethgelert to Waenfawr, Llanberis, Dinorwie, Pentir, Bethesda, Capel Curig, Bettws-y-coed, and Dolyddelen—the villages which surround Snowdonia—the revival has already spread. Like a belt of fire, it encircles the mighty mountains, and whatever *natural* ice and snow may be found on any of their high peaks, or in their craggy recesses, there is but little *moral* ice now left which has not felt, in some degree, the melting power of this gracious influence.

There is yet one county left unnoticed—the last, but not the least in importance—the county of Anglesea. This little island has long been remarkable for the number of its sanctuaries, its communicants, and its Sabbath-schools. Not a little has been said respecting its liberality to the

Bible Society, averaging nearly fourpence each, from its fifty thousand inhabitants. *Now* it bids fair to increase in all these things. From Menai Bridge to Holyhead, from Newborough to Amlwch, from Linas Point to Llanddona Head, along that coast rendered so sadly memorable by the wreck of the *Royal Charter*, the revival spirit is felt, and a great moral revolution is now being effected in the hearts and lives of many of its inhabitants.*

When we speak of the EXTENT of the Welsh Revival, we mean something more than that it covers a large surface of country ; we mean to intimate that it embraces, more or less, all sections of the Christian Church. In addition to the Established Church, Wales has its Nonconformist bodies, such as the *old* Dissenters, consisting of Congregationalists and Baptists, and the *more modern* Dissenters, called the Wesleyans and the Calvinistic Methodists.† The latter are supposed to be the most numerous. They owe their very existence to the great revival in the last century, under the

---

* Little did those numerous Christian travellers know when they passed through this county on their way to Ireland during the summer and autumn of last year, to witness the operations of God's Holy Spirit in Ulster, that on either side of the line along which they were passing, there were equal wonders of grace and mercy being wrought by the influences of the self-same Spirit. But even had they known it, the difference of language would have presented an insurmountable barrier in the way of free intercourse with the people.

† Sometimes called Lady Huntingdon's Connexion, and sometimes Welsh Presbyterians. In common language, the Christian communities in Wales are described as, (1.) Churchmen, (2.) Dissenters, by which is meant the Independents, (3.) Baptists, (4.) Methodists, that is, the Calvinistic section, the only Methodists known in the principality for many years, and (5.) the Wesleyans. There are also a few congregations of Unitarians, Primitive Methodists, and Friends.

extraordinary ministry of Rowlands, Harries, and others, and became dissenters, in the first instance, more from necessity than choice. The good clergymen and laymen who laid the foundation of this great body of Christians laboured far and wide for the good of souls. They were revivalists indeed, and God honoured their work by adding His blessing. This denomination has been often favoured with revivals. They are thus favoured now, but it is not confined to them. All the orthodox denominations of Dissenters are awakened, and their numbers are greatly multiplied. In many of the parish churches too, where the gospel is preached with earnestness, and where the minister, with his congregation of faithful men, seeks an outpouring of the Holy Spirit, that blessing is graciously vouchsafed. A venerable clergyman, long a faithful witness for the truth, to whose church many additions have been made during this revival, is said to have expressed himself thus at a prayer-meeting, "I thank Thee, O God, that Thou hast visited our old church before I die." Many other clergymen, who are like-minded, have had similar occasion for using the language of thankfulness and joy.

CHAPTER II.

GENERAL statements require illustration, and the broad assertions already made should be fortified by documentary evidence. A selection, therefore, from a very ample correspondence will now be presented. We shall take the two great divisions of the principality, with some regard to the arrangement of counties and the dates of letters. We begin with

CARDIGANSHIRE.

A clergyman writes from Glamorganshire :—" I have glorious news to send you, news which I am sure will make your heart leap for joy. The Spirit of God is working powerfully throughout the two counties of Cardigan and Caermarthen in South Wales. The services in the churches and chapels on week-days and Sabbath-days are crowded. *Hundreds* are coming over to the Lord's side, and there seems to be an extraordinary work of grace going forward amongst us. There is no enthusiasm, but a deep, profound, and awfully solemn impression prevails."

Another clergyman writes :—" There is a revival (thank God for it !) in the upper part of Cardiganshire. Sinners, and some very notorious ones, are flocking to the Church by the scores, and I may say *hundreds*. Do not misunderstand me when I say *the Church*, as meaning the Church of England exclusively, but *the Church of Christ*, including different denominations. I am not so bigoted as to think that the Church of God is not among the Methodists, &c., though they differ from us in *minor* points. I feel my heart full of gratitude when I think of the revival—of prodigals returning home to their Father's house, and feasting on the precious Sacrifice of Calvary! They say that there are upwards of three hundred who have joined the Church at Aberystwith, and there are scores and scores who have joined religion in the neighbouring chapels. I was at Tregaron last Sunday evening, and it was delightful to be there; indeed, it was a glorious meeting, but only five joined there that night. Mr Hughes has received between forty and fifty new converts in the course of last month."

In April 1859, a correspondent says—

" In the town of Aberystwith about four hundred members have been added to the Calvinistic Methodist Church alone. Several of the most ungodly people of the town have been converted. Eight publicans have taken down their signs, and become teetotallers. The work commenced here one Friday night, when Mr David Morgan was preaching. A few agreed privately to meet on the Saturday afternoon to pray for a blessing on the services of the Sabbath. The report soon spread that such a meeting was to be held, and, although it was a market day, most of the shops were closed, and the chapel filled to overflowing."

A few months after the commencement of the revival in Cardiganshire, the Rev. T. Edwards, of Penllwyn, thus writes :—" Many of the ministers of this county have received a new spirit, and prosecute their work with fresh vigour. It is clear that God works through them in a marvellous manner. Indeed, all the ministers and elders, and other good people, have become more serious and earnest than usual. The feelings and general demeanour of the inhabitants of the county change rapidly. Religion and the present revival is the subject of conversation amongst all classes, and it produces a great impression upon them. At the same time, we have our fears lest the work should prove superficial, and that we are bringing men into the visible Church of Christ who have not been convinced of sin, and converted by the Spirit of God. Most of us, however, have lost these fears, and we cannot avoid coming to the conclusion that God is at work, saving the souls of men. We see that something awfully strong takes hold of the minds of the people. Some, after they are deeply wounded under the ministry, attempt to go away. We have seen numbers with weeping eyes leaving the house of God, but unable to go further than the door; they feel compelled to return again, and offer themselves as candidates for admission into the Church. In some cases entire families have done this. You might see, at the close of the public service, twenty or thirty of the worst characters remaining behind, to be spoken to and prayed for. They appear as if they had been shot by the truth. They are as easily managed as lambs. Some who had persecuted the revival have been led to cry, ' What must we do to be saved?' We have known persons who, having entered the chapel to scoff, remain to pray. Not far from this place, a young man, about fifteen years of age, and belonging to an irreligious family, after he was converted introduced domestic worship. His father and brother-in-law were inclined to ridicule; they told him he would require a new prayer each time, and that he must not use the same prayer more than once. By the following Sunday evening the two were arrested by the power of God's word, to the great joy of the youth.

"The additions to the churches in a very short period have been incredibly numerous. Now, at the end of February (1859,) we could name more than twenty churches, each of which has received an addition of one hundred members, and several have received more than two hundred each. In many neighbourhoods, very few persons remain who have not made a profession of religion. There are considerable additions to the parish churches, (where the ministers have church meetings or societies,) and to the Independents, Baptists, and Wesleyans. About three thousand have been added to the Calvinistic Methodists alone. The fire is spreading still."

The Rev. W. Evans of Aberayron bears the following testimony :—

"So far as the *externals* of religion are concerned, they were never in a more prosperous state than before the dawning of this revival But, as for the *internals*—the spiritual temple—these were far from being in a satisfactory condition. The spirituality of religion was a strange thing to many who were content with its mere outward profession. But how different is the state of things now amongst us ! Language can hardly express the vast good God has graciously done among us ! We are at a loss to find words to express our gratitude to Him for such a blessed visitation as we had in this outpouring of His Spirit ! A happy change is everywhere observed—our prayer-meetings are become crowded, and a powerful spirit of prayer has laid hold of the Churches. The number of praying and prayerful people has marvellously increased.

"One of the most striking characteristics of this movement is its effects on young people, and even on children. The words of the prophet are abundantly fulfilled in these days, 'For I will pour water upon him that is thirsty, and floods upon the dry ground : I will pour my Spirit upon thy seed, and my blessing upon thine offspring, and they shall spring up as among the grass, as willows by the water-courses.' The youth of our congregations are nearly all the subjects of deep religious impressions. Many of them seem as if filled with the spirit of prayer. Very young people, yea, children from ten to fourteen years of age, gather together to hold prayer-meetings, and pray very fer-vently. I have never witnessed so much willingness in candidates for church membership to put on the *entire* form of the Christian religion, and exercise themselves in all religious duties, as I do now. We have invariably im-pressed on the male candidates the importance of *family religion,* and they invariably and promptly promised to establish family worship. We have never seen such an outburst of feeling as we have in many that have recently been brought under religious impressions. To hear some of them stating what they have passed through is truly affecting ; and their earnest, simple, and fervent prayers quite overcome us. Some, after sustaining a severe struggle with their heart-convictions for many days and nights without sleep and without rest, happily at last find peace in Christ to their weary souls, and resolve henceforth to live in Christ and to Him. It has been the practice among us, for some months past, to hold church-meetings after almost every service, to which inquirers have been invited, and are even exhorted to stay with the Church. We have known of many, after mustering all their strength to go out after the sermon or prayer-meeting, finding it too hard to go further than the door, being constrained by their convictions to turn back and join the Church. In a word, in these days something extraordinary has seized upon the mass of the people, for the thing is a wonder to all, a joy to many, and a terror to others.

"Among the fruits of this great revival, the following facts are prominent :—We find many that had led a long life of open rebellion against religion, and everything spiritually good, numbered now with the family of God. Some of the worst characters have been made new creatures, confessing they never knew the comforts of life till now; and some thank God on their knees that they have enjoyed more happiness in one hour of communion with God, than they had during many years of wasteful life, during which they had expended their thousands in the service of sin.

"It would be a difficult thing for me now to fix upon the probable number of converts. About two hundred have been added to the churches under my care."

We conclude our notice of Cardiganshire with a letter, recently received from the Venerable Archdeacon Hughes, dated

"LLANBADARN VICARAGE, NEAR ABERYSTWITH,
13th February 1860.

"MY DEAR SIR,—In compliance with your request, I beg to send you a few lines respecting the late revival in this neighbourhood. Between Aberystwith and Llanbadarn the Established Church has received new members to the amount of two hundred and sixty. They offered themselves apparently in a very proper state of mind—exhibiting nothing enthusiastic in their manner, but with proper impressions of the weight and importance of what they were doing. As might be expected, many in various places have gone back to the world, while many thousands give evidence of sincerity which ought to beget gratitude and praise.

" The religious revival, on the whole, I firmly believe, has been a great and extensive blessing to the principality. Multitudes of the most thoughtless characters have become, in outward conduct at least, correct and respectable."

CAERMARTHENSHIRE.

In reference to this county, the Rev. R. Phillips, of Llandovery, writes as follows :—

" It is supposed that about three thousand persons have been added to the Calvinistic Methodist Churches in this county during the past year. Some of the greatest drunkards in some neighbourhoods give evidence of a change of heart by a change of life. The old people say that there is more of God in this revival than they ever saw in any similar movement. It is quite clear that a work has been done which none but God could accomplish. In some places the cause of religion had nearly died away, but now those places are quickened. The churches, which were small, have received a large accession of members, and new life runs through the whole.

" The town of *Llandovery* has not been awakened to the same degree as some other places ; but still all the denominations have increased the number of their communicants during the year. We have had a few drops, and all the churches are longing for the heavy shower of Divine influences.

" There has been a most powerful revival at *Cilycwm*, and about two hundred souls have been added to one church. The prayer-meetings held once every week were greatly blest, and the sermon preached by the Rev. O. Thomas, of London, on a Sunday afternoon in the month of August last, will never be forgotten. The effects were overwhelming, and many were added as the result. Conversions have been numerous at *Rhandir-mwyn* and *Goshen.* More than one hundred persons have been admitted into church-fellowship at *Cwrt*, in the *Cothy* valley. Before the revival the members were but forty, and now they are one hundred and sixty. Indeed, there are only half-a-dozen persons in this valley who do not make a profession of religion.

" The Independents at *Ffald-y-brenin* and *Crûg-y-bar*, and the Baptists at *Bethel* and *Salem* in the same district, have received a large accession of members. It may be said that nothing is now left to the devil but a few gleanings ; the large sheaves are in possession of the Lord of the harvest.

" At *Llansawel* more than one hundred and twenty persons have been admitted, and the services continue to be attended very numerously. The congregation at *Talley* has greatly increased, and many scores have been added to the Church. Amongst the converted are the greatest drunkards in the parish : men who never went to a fair or a market without returning home perfectly drunk. But as far as we can judge at present, there is a thorough change in these characters. The converts at *Llansadwrn* are chiefly young people, and all the religious communities of this place have been strengthened by new members.

" Although there is nothing very powerful at *Llanddeusant* or *Mothvey*, there have been considerable additions. The week of prayer, in compliance with the request of the missionaries in India, was a remarkable week at the former place. At a church meeting held after the service, the entire congregation remained, placing themselves for the time in the condition of inquirers. At *Llangadock* and *Llandilo* considerable numbers have been added to the various places of worship, and at the latter place to the communion of the parish church. At *Llangathen*, also, a great work has been effected. Amongst the candidates at this place an octogenarian presented himself. The following was a part of the conversation between him and the minister. When the latter said,—'You have been very long in the service of sin and Satan?' the old man replied, 'Too long by far, sir.' 'Do you not think,' said the minister, 'that your old master will be angry with you for quitting his service?' 'I think not,' was the simple reply. 'What makes you think so?' said the minister. 'Well,' said the old man, 'I gave him notice about a year ago that I intended leaving him.'

"If we pass on to *Cross Inn* we shall find a great change in many persons. At *Llanfynydd* the Holy Spirit has been poured out, and blasphemers are now found humble petitioners at the throne of mercy. The following places have shared largely in the blessings of the present awakening:— Rhyd-cymmerau, Bont-ynys-wen, Brechfa, Abergorlech, Nantcaredig, Capel Dewi, Llanarthney, and Llanddarog.

"There is no great stir as yet at Caermarthen, but the meetings for prayer, congregationally and unitedly, are increasing in interest, and some additions have been made. At Newcastle Emlyn, Closygraig, New Inn, Llanpumpsaint, Pantgwyn, Cwmdwyfran, Conwil, Llandefeiliog, Kidwelly, Pembrey, and Llanelly, a work similar to the above has been accomplished, and in many of these, as elsewhere, backsliders have been reclaimed and restored to their lost privileges.

"There are many other places which might have been named; and although I cannot give particulars of other denominations, it may be said thankfully that the revival is almost universal in this county. Our joyful song is, 'The Lord hath done great things for us, whereof we are glad.'"

" From these general statements it would be easy for me to pass to particular instances of the work of grace in the conversion of notorious sinners.

" The head of a family was recently received into communion. He had a wife and nine children, but on account of his intemperate habits they were sunk in poverty. None of them attended public worship. He was, however, induced to become a total abstainer. He took the pledge, and kept it. This led him to attend the chapel and the Sunday school.* He was impressed under the word— convictions laid hold of him—with weeping and supplication he sought a place amongst the people of God. His wife and children also are the subjects of a great moral and social change. The change in this family has produced the most salutary impression on large numbers.

" A large farmer in this county, who had been addicted to drunkenness for many years, but who had a religious wife, has recently been brought to submit to the yoke of Christ. He felt it was his duty to set up family worship, but was kept back by various considerations. Even on the morning he fully resolved to commence, the presence of a carpenter who worked for him, and who was a persecutor and scoffer, made him hesitate. He was about to give it up even after he had opened the Bible. He turned to this scoffer and said to him, ' Will you read a chapter and pray ? It is as much your duty as mine, although you make no profession of religion.' This completely weakened his power to scoff. He bowed his head, and the farmer proceeded with reading and prayer, being his first attempt to honour the Lord under his own roof. This service produced serious impressions on the carpenter's mind, and the result

* In Wales, adults, as well as children, attend the Sunday schools, and are expected to do so.

is, that he also has yielded to the claims of religion, and
now rejoices 'in the cross of our Lord Jesus Christ.'

"I ought to add that the leaders and office-bearers in
the churches throughout the country have been greatly
awakened—the spirit of *doing* good has fallen upon them.
They are like so many home missionaries—they preach to
the people wherever they meet them, in the streets or elsewhere, in the spirit of the injunction, ' Compel them to
come in.'"

The following communication, dated Feb. 25, 1860, is
from the Rev. J. Griffiths, Vicar of Llandilo-fawr :—

"I have delayed replying to your letter with the hope
that I should have a more copious report to furnish in
respect to the wonderful movement in Wales, generally
termed 'revivals.' During last year, and indeed in this,
we have had a great accession to our church, and the impression on my mind is, that the hand of the Lord is
plainly visible throughout. What can the sceptical world
say when you see a stalwart, athletic man, in the vigour of
robust manhood, whose previous life was that of a thoughtless man, not caring for his soul nor his family, brought to
his knees, and crying out, like the prodigal, 'I have sinned
against heaven and before thee,' and continuing faithful to
Christ and His gospel for nearly a whole year?

"This is only one instance of many that I could mention.

"There are many things connected with this movement,
like everything else, which you cannot soberly approve ; but
I am firmly persuaded that the Almighty is opening the
sluices of grace and pouring out streams of blessings on the
churches of all denominations.

"The Union meetings seem to be blessed to a great
extent in the neighbourhood of Newcastle Emlyn. When-

ever two or three are gathered together to address the throne of grace, believing, in the name of Jesus, that they shall receive the blessing asked for, they are heard, and the place is too confined to accommodate the crowds that assemble in consequence. God seems to honour prayer-meetings more than any other means of grace in this movement. If the churches—or may I not rather say the Church of Christ—were to petition the House of Mercy, God's Bethesda, with that simplicity and importunity which the Scriptures indicate and encourage, I verily believe that we should succeed in making a paradise again of our globe. It is the narrow-mindedness and self-exaltation of the Christian Church that ties up the hands which are over-flowing with blessings to man; the *practical* influence and *obedience* of faith which appear to follow this revival restrains the tongue of the sceptic and drives the scoffer to a corner."

Abergwili, near *Caermarthen*. The Rev. D. C. Jones writes, February 29 :—" We have been visited with a larger measure of the Spirit's influences than usual. It came suddenly 'like a rushing mighty wind,' and that apparently when the churches little expected it.

" The first indications were observed in the month of May last, when the prayer-meetings were better attended, and larger numbers came to the public services on the Lord's day, and more punctually than usual. It was evident, from the earnest attention paid to the sermons and to every part of the service, that a deep feeling pervaded the congregation. I endeavoured to deepen and to draw out this earnest feeling by preaching from Hosea xiii. 13. This was done in my two congregations and with marked effect. During the three succeeding months I had the inexpressible pleasure of giving the right hand of fellowship to upwards of two hundred persons.   I am thankful to be able to say that, with few exceptions, they give me abundant satisfaction.

"This religious movement is somewhat different from the former revivals with which Wales has been favoured. We have had no loud exhibition of feeling, but rather a strong current of inward emotions, finding vent in floods of tears.   I hope it is not a transient thing, but, on the contrary, that this 'Gad' will be followed by a 'troop.'   There is already a considerable change in the aspect of the neighbourhoods where the revival has prevailed.   The temperance movement gathers strength, and some of the public-houses are gasping for breath, as though they were in the *last struggle*."

GLAMORGANSHIRE.

Out of many communications from this county, the following is selected.   It is from the pen of a minister who has been much honoured of God in this and in former revivals :—

"LLANHARAN, *Feb.* 10, 1860.

" I have the greatest pleasure in stating that this locality has been blessed with a most powerful religious awakening for the last twelve months.   Considering the scanty population of these parts, compared with the towns, works, and mineral districts, the revival here is regarded as one of the most wonderful and powerful hitherto known in Wales. The hand of the Lord is clearly revealed, and multitudes are added unto the Lord.   The circumstances under which the heavenly gale began to blow, are as follows :—At our annual assembly, held at Aberdare, in June 1858, it was proposed and unanimously resolved, that the first Sunday in the following August should be set apart by all the churches and congregations of our association in the four counties — viz., Glamorgan, Monmouth, Brecknock, and Radnor—to pray unitedly and earnestly for the outpouring of God's Spirit. I went home, and stated the resolution to my people, and some unusual feelings thrilled through the minds of all present. When the stated Sabbath arrived, we were blessed with remarkable earnestness at the throne of grace for the descent of the Holy Spirit to revive the Church and convert the world. Ever since that memorable Sabbath, the prayer-meetings presented a new aspect,—they gradually increased in warmth and number during the following months. This continued to February last, when it pleased Jehovah to pour down His Spirit from on high, as on the day of Pentecost. Then anxious inquirers came forward in dozens, some under strong mental emotions, perceiving their lost state as sinners; and shortly they received relief to their minds by exercising faith in the merits of our Lord and Saviour Jesus Christ. At this period it was advisable to publish prayer-meetings daily, and the attendance constantly increased for months, and continues doing so to the present time. Our chapels and other places of worship are overcrowded. At the close of each meeting we announced a Society (church-meeting), and new converts came forward daily. The number of these at present in our churches amounts to several hundreds. The churches are generally doubled in number, and new inquirers are continually coming forward. The heavenly fire still continues to burn, and the flames have spread throughout the county at large. All religious denominations are cordially united in social prayer-meetings, and the descent of Divine influence amongst us is evident. The writer of these lines (to God be the praise) has had the great honour of giving the right hand of fellowship to more than six hundred and

fifty new candidates for membership in our churches in this
district since February last; and that in a comparatively
small circle too.   The revival is progressing and spreading
universally in this new year throughout the towns, iron-
works, villages, and hamlets of Glamorganshire, especially
in that part of the county called '*The Vale.*'   Those parts
of the county which were usually considered to be the
darkest, and where the inhabitants were most absorbed
in worldly cares, are now generally roused and awakened,
and 'raised from the dead,' and Christ himself gives them
light.   We have no cases of physical prostration; persons
are not struck to the ground here, as in Ireland and
Scotland; but we have many cases of very sudden and
powerful changes in those who have discovered their lost
state, while pursuing their several avocations on the mountains, and who on the spot were led to cry for mercy.
Many of the old standard hearers of the gospel are led to
seek pardoning grace.   They now seem as though they were
born over again; and the very sound of their voices moves
the whole congregation into tears, and exclamations of
'Hallelujah!' universally burst forth.   Now and then we
witness persons, under the influence of saving grace, leap-
ing in spiritual joy.   We have converts whose ages vary
from nine years to eighty, and in some instances eighty-
four years of age; and both young and old give evidence of
spiritual life.   The new-born babes in Christ form themselves into divers prayer-meetings, and their supplications
at the throne of grace are remarkably earnest; they sometimes pray for their friends and relatives by name, and so
earnest is the prayer, that they will not leave the mercy-
seat until they prevail.   The result is, that others (ready to
perish) are continually brought in at the great trumpet-
sound of salvation.   'The Lord hath done great things for

us, whereof we are glad.' Thousands, since the commencement of this revival, have been converted and brought
home to God amongst our own denomination in these
parts, numbering more than twenty congregations. Other
denominations of the Christian Church throughout this
county, especially in '*The Vale*,' have been blessed with
the same wonderful results. This period must assuredly
be the dawn of the glorious Millennium.

WILLIAM GRIFFITHS."

The iron districts of Merthyr, Dowlais, and more especially
of Aberdare, have had extensive awakenings. The Rev. W.
Edwards, in concluding a long and interesting account of
the revival, more particularly in his own large congregation,
says,—" In its relation to us, the revival came after a year's
longing, praying, and labouring for it. It has subdued
some of the oldest hearers and those who had long remained
obstinate. This revival is distinguished by solemnity of
feeling and great earnestness in prayer. There is something in it which leads the people to make every effort to
gain others. As an illustration of the latter remark, I may
give the following instance. There is on Hirwaen Common
a spot of ground which has long since been possessed by
Sabbath-breakers. To this place large numbers resorted to
play at '*pitch-and-toss*' and other idle games. It was in
vain that the *police* endeavoured to scatter them. On a
certain Sunday, however, three of our young men, with their
Bibles in their pockets, went to the place, and by the time
they arrived the people were in full play. The young men
were laughed at, despised, and mocked, but they were not
to be discouraged. They felt their responsibility. They
used the sword of the Spirit. A chapter was read—prayer
followed, and in a short time the company broke up—they

decamped, leaving the game unfinished, and the money behind. They have never gone again, and on the following Sunday one of the party said that he had done with it for ever, and that he and his companions intended going to the Sunday school."

The religious awakening in this district is thus described by the Rev. T. Rees, of Beaufort, in October last :—" The churches at Aberdare have been blessed with a most powerful revival this year. From one thousand to one thousand two hundred members have been added to the Independent denomination in the parish of Aberdare alone, within the last six months. The churches throughout the whole manufacturing districts from Swansea to Pontypool are to some extent favoured with a revival."

From Swansea and the neighbourhood, we hear that the Spirit of the Lord is at work ; more powerfully, perhaps, in the country places than in the town itself. The great prayer week was well observed. The Rev. W. Williams remarks :—" There was a vast amount of feeling at several of the services. On Friday evening there was loud sobbing heard throughout the chapel, and one young person who had been a source of trouble to her parents screamed aloud. Another went home and burnt all her ' London Journals.' . . . . . . As to results, we have seen some already, and expect more. There is an evident increase of earnestness in Christians of all denominations. Ministers pray and preach as they never did before."

BRECKNOCKSHIRE.

At a place called *Llanwrtyd*, and in the neighbouring parishes throughout the hundred of Builth, the revival has been very powerful for many months past. It commenced amongst the Calvinistic Methodists. The first outburst is thus described :—

"For some time the old members felt that the Church was not as of old, and their hearts longed for a new visitation. On a week-day evening, a prayer-meeting was held in a dwelling-house in one of the dingles running up between the lofty and barren mountains of the neighbourhood. In this meeting something strange and powerful was experienced. The young people could not refrain from singing. They sang all the way home. It was not common singing. The new tunes, cold, formal, and straitened as most of them are, had no share in it ; it was the old, heavenly, unctuous heart-singing of days gone by. Its source was joy and heavenly peace in the heart ; bursting as an overflowing well, its streams could not be stopped. The people of the village heard the singing. One of the old people, who had long sighed for the revival, said, ' There it is. That is the very thing that I have longed for. Thank God !' The singers reached the village, and the feeling spread like wild fire, till most of the people were singing and praying. On the following Sunday a great many sought admission into the church. Strong men were overpowered, and began to pray and praise aloud. The children also partook largely of the blessed influence, and about a dozen of them began to pray and sing together, and continued to do so for hours. Two of these were the children of a publican ; one was, I believe, ten, and the other twelve years old. They went home, praising the Redeemer aloud. In the house they took hold of their father, one on each side, still praising God, and imploring him to join them. At last he asked them to desist, saying that they had sung enough. They replied that they had not sung enough, and at last the father was constrained to join them. The children and young people began to hold prayer-meetings, from house to house, and the revival continued to spread. Many people came from great distances to attend the meetings, and to witness the effects. Most of these experienced its power, and, returning home new men, they became instrumental in commencing the good work in their own neighbourhoods."

The Rev. Lewis Davies, a minister in this neighbourhood, says, " We have proceeded cautiously, not wishing to take the lead of the Holy Spirit, or to lag behind, when we had evidences of the Spirit's work on the minds of the people. The young people, those who had been brought up religiously, were the first affected. Since then the work has spread. Our church-meetings have been held separately, and not in connexion with other services, so as not to avail ourselves of any excitement. More than fifty members have been received at Gorwydd, and both at Bont and Llangammarch the churches have doubled their numbers. Thus far they go on well."

At the close of last year the Rev. T. Rees writes :— " Many of the students in the Independent College at Brecon are full of the revival fire, and their Sabbath visits to the neighbouring churches are eminently blessed. Many churches in Brecknockshire are now experiencing the powers of the world to come, to a greater degree than they ever did before. The ancient Congregational church at *Llangattock*, near Crickhowell, after a long and dreary winter, is now beginning to enjoy ' times of refreshing from the presence of the Lord.' Several congregations in the neighbourhood of Builth have had their numbers doubled within the last few weeks. *Cwmcamlais* is a small secluded place between the mountains, about six miles from Brecon. The adult population of the valley does not exceed one hundred and fifty. The Congregational church, which is the only religious society in the district, consisted of forty members. Some of them are very old, and have adorned their religious profession for more than sixty years. These aged Christians have, for a long time, been longing and praying for a gracious visit from the Lord previous to their departure, and on the 11th of this month (December) their prayers were answered. A most powerful and irresistible influence was felt by the whole congregation. Since that day, from twenty to thirty have joined the church, and the earnest expectation and prayers of all the friends of religion are, that the Lord will continue to pour down His Holy Spirit until every soul in the valley is brought to the Saviour." Mr Stephens, the minister, in a letter received from him this week, says :— " The Lord has graciously visited the small church at *Cwmcamlais*. The old members are quite overcome with joy, and the hearers flock into the church. Above twenty have been united to us this week. Come to see us, and give us two or three sermons. It does not matter what day you come—the Sabbath, or a week-day—for *every day is a Sabbath with us now*. The people cannot think of doing anything but feed their cattle, and attend the prayer-meetings." *

PEMBROKESHIRE.

The population of this county is partly Welsh and partly English. There is considerable religious activity amongst all denominations, and unmistakeable signs of revival in many parts. With few exceptions, the movement is silent, but the tide keeps advancing. Churches which had been

---

* Under date of March 24, it is stated by the Rev. W. Griffiths, after a visit to this place, " All the inhabitants are now turned to the Lord."

dormant for years, and into which the reception of a fresh communicant was a rare occurrence, are now greatly awakened. A correspondent says :—" Pembrokeshire has been favoured with gracious visitations. Aged Christians have been 'renewed in the spirit of their minds,' as evidenced by their prayers and experiences. In some places powerful awakenings have been felt—so strong that the awakened parties have been unable to remain silent in the services. Perhaps the most remarkable movement is at *Trevine*, where the members have been more than doubled. I happened to be there on the Sunday previous to the week set apart for prayer, at the request of the missionaries in India. On that day and the following week there was much of the presence of God with His people. Day by day the meetings were held ; many of the persons who engaged publicly in prayer were, a few months previously, the faithful servants of the enemy. Their gift in prayer was almost miraculous. I never spent such a Sabbath in my life. I was there again on Saturday night last, on my way to St David's. There is a considerable awakening in other places, and my opinion is, that if we had more life and earnestness in the pulpit, there would be far more life and holiness in the congregations."

RADNORSHIRE.

This small county of 25,000 inhabitants has long since ceased to be Welsh in language. For many reasons, it has not been so well supplied with an enlightened ministry as some other counties. To supply this lack, home missionaries* have been located at different points ; and it is gratifying to be able to state that signs of an awakening have

---

* The Calvinistic Methodists of South Wales support three home missionaries in this county.

been witnessed within the last few months in some of the towns, and in several of the villages.

A correspondent at *Rhayader* writes—" One of the most remarkable things is the disappearance of drunkenness. Some of the most noted drunkards have not only joined the Total Abstinence Society, but also the Church of Christ, and for some months past their conduct has been irreproachable. We do indeed ' rejoice,' but it is ' with trembling.' "

The Rev. S. Roberts of *Penybont* writes, in January— " The revival is only beginning with us ; " and then proceeds to give an account of the deep interest awakened by the special prayer-meetings at the different villages on his station. At a very small village he had already received fourteen members, and looked forward to the pleasure of receiving shortly an equal number. Some of the conversions which had taken place were very striking. He says, " A very remarkable character presented himself as a candidate for membership. According to his own account, he had been ' a ringleader in the devil's army, and had passed the last twenty years of his life without a ray of light or hope.' Though he was the son of a pious father, he never attended the means of grace. Since his change, he has been zealous in the service of his new Master. He goes from house to house to reason with his old companions respecting the folly of sin. On one occasion he met two young men, who had been his associates in wickedness, and immediately addressed them on the sinfulness and danger of the life they led. At first they were inclined to laugh, but his earnestness overcame them, and they wept. He took out his Bible, read and prayed on the spot. The young men testified that they felt as they had never felt before. The conversion of this man has produced a great

sensation in the neighbourhood.   He is a farmer, and forty
years of age."

But the strongest religious movement in this county is
felt at *Presteign, Knighton,* and the neighbourhood.   The
following extracts from a letter written by the Rev. T. L.
Davies, the Baptist minister at the first-named place, will
be read with interest :—

"The first symptoms of the work appeared about four
months ago in a *revival of the spirit of prayer.* That branch
of the Church of Christ over which I preside resolved about
that time to hold prayer-meetings every night, to plead
with the Lord for the outpouring of the Holy Spirit.
'Oh,' was our cry, 'that Thou wouldest rend the heavens,
that Thou wouldest come down, that the mountains might
flow down at Thy presence !' These meetings were attended
with unusual power.   We felt that God of a truth was with
us, and that He was about displaying His power in the
salvation of many souls.

"In the latter end of November it was proposed that we
should hold *united prayer-meetings.*   This met with the
hearty approval of all the Dissenters in the town, and the
Baptists, Primitive Methodists, and the Wesleyans soon
met successively, at their respective chapels, without any
semblance of sectarianism.

"All deeply felt the necessity of prayer—of united prayer
and effort for the conversion of precious souls ; and hence
the house of prayer became a delightful resort.   We all
wished to pray.   We all delighted to pray.   We were all
impelled to pray, by an unseen Power.

"Those who had, a few weeks before, very little inclination for prayer-meetings, and very seldom attended them.
now flocked to them, and are among the foremost in promoting the work.

"This had a marked influence on the world; for, in addition to the earnest spirit of prayer which prevailed, they saw, that an earnest spirit of *united prayer* and *united effort* for their salvation prevailed. They saw that it was no longer the movement of a party or of a sect; but that all the true from all the sects had but one common object in view, namely, the conversion of their souls—the glory of Christ.

"Many now became deeply concerned about their souls, and earnestly sought the Lord for mercy, through the blood of Jesus, shed for the remission of sins. It became evident to all that our prayers were answered—that the Spirit was poured out from on high; for almost every night were seen the tears of the penitent, were heard the sighs and sobs of the mourner and broken-hearted, and the cries of those who saw their lost condition.

"It is impossible for me to enter into details, or inform you of half of what we have felt, and heard, and seen during this precious season of refreshing from the presence of the Lord. But some of the meetings and the cases of conversion deserve special mention. We had an extraordinary meeting at the Primitive Methodist chapel on New-year's eve. Several of the brethren prayed, and others addressed the meeting, and afterwards some minutes were spent in *silent prayer*. We felt at this time as if the glory of the Lord was passing by, whilst we were in the cleft of the rock. I am not aware that there were any conversions that night, but *every one* at the meeting was more or less affected—many very deeply.

"At a crowded meeting, held at the Baptist chapel, the following Friday night; after a sermon by Mr L. Cowdell, and another by the Rev. Mr Huff, and a few words by myself, twelve came forward in deep distress, and eight found peace. 'Being justified by faith,' they 'had peace with God through our Lord Jesus Christ.' On the following Sunday night, at the same place, ten more appeared in the deepest distress about their soul's salvation, and most of them found peace. But I never felt the influence of the Holy Spirit so powerful as on the following Tuesday night, at the same chapel. After several of the brethren had engaged in prayer, and a short address had been delivered, an invitation was given to all who were concerned about their soul's salvation, to come forward to the communion table. Nine moved out whilst we were directing them to the Saviour. The Holy Ghost descended upon us ; not, indeed, 'as a rushing mighty wind,' yet as the gentle zephyr, till it filled the whole place. So powerful was the influence that none of us could speak for some minutes. We all gave vent to our feelings in floods of joyful tears. We met the next night at the Wesleyan chapel. After a very impressive sermon by the Rev. Mr Kirkland, an invitation was given to all anxious inquirers to come forward to the communion rail. A young woman came forward in the greatest conceivable distress ; after her came a young lady in like distress ; and following them came an elderly lady. After we had directed them to Jesus and had prayed for them, we rose up and were about to dismiss the congregation, when the last said to the first, 'Why, Mary, is it you?' It was her servant, and the second that came was 'her daughter. Thus three were led from the same house to seek the Lord without any previous knowledge of each other's intention. They did not find peace that night, but the three are now rejoicing in the Lord Jesus.

"I am not able to inform you how many have been converted, or who have professed to be, but a very large number (taking into consideration the population) have been, whilst many have been received into the fellowship of the Wesleyans and Primitive Methodists. I had the pleasure, on the second Sabbath of last month, of baptizing thirty-four 'in the name of the Father, and of the Son, and of the Holy Ghost,' and there are upwards of sixty more seeking our fellowship. Seven found peace at the Wesleyan chapel last Wednesday night.

"Nor is this influence confined to the town—it more or less pervades the whole neighbourhood. The revival is very powerfully felt at *Stansbatch*, a little place about four miles from here. Upwards of thirty have been recently converted there. We have union prayer-meetings there also. At one of these, not long ago, eleven declared themselves on the Lord's side. At this meeting, the wife of a man who had been recently converted meekly said that she had found peace in the Lord Jesus. *She was converted in answer to her husband's prayers.* He was asked to tell the meeting how the Lord had answered his prayers. He did so with tears of joy flowing down his cheeks, which deeply affected us all. He said, that since he had determined to follow Christ, his wife very much opposed him, and was the source of much trouble and anxiety to him. She would often say, 'I can't think what you want at those meetings.' He said, I resolved to pray for her, and one evening when I was conducting family worship, and reading the twelfth chapter of the Acts of the Apostles, she cried out in deep distress, 'O Charles, what shall I do? what shall I do? will you pray for me?' He said, 'Yes, with all my heart.' They knelt down and continued in earnest prayer till ten o'clock, when it pleased the Lord to speak peace to her soul. At the same meeting, a little girl came forward, seeking the Lord in deep distress. When we were directing her to the Saviour, a man was heard sobbing and weeping bitterly, and crying aloud for mercy. 'O God,' he said, 'have mercy upon me; oh! save me or I die.' He was the little girl's father. He rose and moved on to his little daughter, and threw his arms round her neck, and both, weeping and broken-hearted, knelt down, and continued in earnest prayer for about fifteen minutes. The father continued in great distress for many days. At a subsequent meeting he told us, to our great joy, that the Lord had had mercy upon him—that his burden had been removed—that his sins had been forgiven—and that he knew now what it was to rejoice in Jesus."

"*This is the Lord's doing; it is marvellous in our eyes.*" (Psalm cxviii. 23.) *To Him be all the praise!*

"The Lord has poured out His Spirit in this great revival, in answer to the fervent prayers of His people. It is a glorious truth—oh that the Church—the universal Church—realised it—*that the prayer of faith prevails with God!*

"This revival is altogether a REVIVAL OF THE SPIRIT OF PRAYER; it takes its embodied form in CHRISTIAN UNITY.

"These constitute the strength of the Church. Let the Church pray—unitedly pray, and unitedly 'strive for the faith once delivered unto the saints,' and the world will soon feel that Christianity is a power—a power which it is altogether unable to withstand. Let Christianity but be presented, not as it is found in our conventional theology, nor through the medium of a sect, but as it is found in the Book, with genial and loving warmth, and, under the influence of God's Spirit, it will soon move and captivate the world.

> " Let party names no more
> 　　The Christian world o'erspread;
> 　Gentile and Jew, and bond and free,
> 　　*Are one in Christ their Head.*"

" Let the Church—the whole Church say, '*For Zion's sake will I not hold my peace, and for Jerusalem's sake I will not rest, until the righteousness thereof go forth as brightness, and the salvation thereof as a lamp that burneth.*' "

MONMOUTHSHIRE.

This county, though nominally in England, is essentially a part of the principality. The Welsh language is still spoken in a few of the towns, and predominates in some of the country districts, more especially the localities which have become the seat and centre of the great iron works. Here a vast number of people—English, Scotch, Irish, and Welsh—are congregated, and immense efforts have been made for their spiritual benefit both by Churchmen and Dissenters. The revival, in all its power and blessedness, has penetrated the iron and colliery districts. All classes have experienced its effects. Its divine character has been attested by the marvellous change wrought in the habits of thought, and speech, and action of multitudes, and some of them the most abandoned and wicked in the families and neighbourhoods to which they belonged.

The Rev. Thos. Rees, of Beaufort, whose church and congregation have shared largely in the revival blessings, writes, under date of March 7, as follows :—

" The Welsh Congregational churches in the county of Monmouth have, since the spring of last year, enjoyed ' times of refreshing from the presence of the Lord.' There is scarcely a congregation in the whole of the Welsh district of the county which has not been more or less moved. I am not able to furnish you with the exact number added to our churches, but I am certain that at least two thousand have joined our societies since April 1859. There are amongst the converts several above seventy years of age, and many as young as eight years; but the majority is made up of young people from fifteen to thirty.

"The revival in this county is not so powerful and extensive as it is in Cardiganshire, North Wales, and even in some districts of the counties of Brecknock, Caermarthen, and Glamorgan. Still its blessed effects are visible amongst us in the increased spirituality and zeal of professors, the unexampled co-operation and union of Christians 'of all evangelical denominations, the conversion of multitudes of sinners, and the decided improvement of the population generally in their morals.

"The feelings manifested at the public services in this county are not so intense and overpowering as in some other parts of the principality, but occasionally large congregations are bathed in tears.

"The prayer-meetings held in January last, and in which the Independents, the Calvinistic Methodists, the Wesleyans, and in some rare instances the Baptists and the Episcopalians, most heartily joined, have resulted in the addition of large numbers to the churches. Above fifty have joined the church under my care *since the beginning of this year.* The church under the pastoral care of the Rev. E. Jenkins at Rhymney has had above one hundred and fifty added to it during the same period. In some of our churches the awakening is gaining strength from week to week. May the Lord continue to pour down His Spirit until every lost sinner is brought to the Saviour!"

CHAPTER III.

MERIONETHSHIRE.

FROM the fact of the revival having become so general in this county, it is no easy matter to make a selection of illustrative facts and statements out of the materials at our disposal. We will begin with the mountainous districts, and then give instances from some of the towns.

On the 2d of November 1859, the Rev. D. Edwards, rector of Festiniog and Maentwrog, thus writes :—

"MY DEAR FRIEND,—You will doubtless be pleased to learn that the religious movement which has been taking place in various parts of the world at the present time has at length reached the parishes of Festiniog and Maentwrog. About three weeks ago a few young men from Bettws-y-coed came to work in the Festiniog slate-quarries. They were in deep concern about the state of their souls. They came on Monday morning, and their deep distress was observed by several of the quarrymen. They followed their work in this state of mind, occasionally weeping on account of their lost condition as guilty sinners before God. After dinner the following day they were observed by some working people making their way to the top of the hill. Immediately they were followed by all the workmen in that quarry, being about five hundred in number. They halted on the summit of the mountain, and on that spot, under the broad canopy of heaven, they held a prayer-meeting. Whilst they prayed, the Holy Spirit was poured out upon them most abundantly. Nearly all present wept and sobbed aloud. On the same evening they met at their respective places of worship to hold a prayer-meeting. On the following day they met again on the mountain, leaving their work un-heeded ; for by this time the people were in a state of great religious excitement. They met every night during that week at their several places of worship to offer up prayer to Almighty God. The rocks seemed to re-echo the voice of prayer and praise. On the following Saturday those who lived at a distance went to their homes, carrying with them the newly-kindled revival fire, and on the morrow the surrounding churches and chapels were in a blaze ! Our people met at Maentwrog to hold a Saturday-evening prayer-meeting. I attended it, and witnessing the effects already produced upon those who were present, it was announced that another prayer-meeting would be held next morning at eight o'clock. Such a prayer-meeting I never attended. The most ungodly persons present were over-whelmed. We prayed and wept, wept and prayed, until nature was exhausted. Instead of the Sunday-school, as usual, in the afternoon, we met to pray again ; but in the interval at noon all the congregations, church and chapel, met on the brow of a hill above the village *to pray*. It was indeed a glorious meeting while it lasted, which was about one hour and a half, when the rain came down in torrents and dispersed us. The following week there were prayer-meetings every night. I attended one which was held in the open air, at the request of a number of workmen who were engaged in building a new bridge. This was a very large meeting.

" The revival has been making progress ever since. Our

church members, both at Festiniog and Maentwrog, have nearly doubled. When I speak thus of what is doing at these churches, you are to understand that things equally interesting are taking place at all the chapels around us, and perhaps more so in some of them. By far the greater part of the population are become members," &c.

In a communication, dated February 3, 1860, addressed to the Rev. John Venn of Hereford, the same writer enters into further particulars :—

> " FESTINIOG RECTORY, TAN-Y-BWLCH,
> " *January* 3, 1860.

" REVEREND AND DEAR SIR,—The revival in this neighbourhood has been steadily progressing since it broke out about the beginning of last October. There was before that time a considerable difference in the state of feeling among all denominations of Dissenters, as well as the Church people, in these two parishes, even since last August. There was more unction in the prayers and the preaching, more unity among Christians, and a readiness to converse on religious matters generally. Prayer-meetings were multiplied, and held in the open air amongst the quarrymen. Every now and then, some in them would break out and cry for mercy. Several were added to the church during this time. There was great warmth and fervour felt in almost every service held during the months of August and September, but the flame was not kindled till that great meeting on the mountain mentioned in my letter to Mr Phillips. Ever since then, there is hardly a religious meeting of any kind where you do not see the most powerful effects produced on the souls of almost all that attend them. I may say that the revival actually commenced among the quarrymen through the instrumentality of those two young men from Bettws-y-Coed, but there had evidently been a preparatory work going on about here in the hearts of hundreds since last summer. Having heard so much of the revival in Cardiganshire, my native county, I went in May last, for a fortnight, to visit my friends in the neighbourhood of Aberystwith. Having closely examined the revival there, and having made all inquiries about its origin and progress in that locality, I gathered that the principal means blessed of God to create and carry it on was PRAYER, and especially the prayers of the new converts. When I came home, I related to my dear people at Maentwrog as much as I could recollect of what I saw and heard of the revival in Cardiganshire, and begged of them to join me in establishing a weekly meeting for the special purpose of praying for a large outpouring of the Holy Spirit. The very recital in these meetings of what I witnessed in Cardiganshire created a stir among my people, and a great many attended the prayer-meeting for a few times; they, however, cooled down again into their former state of apathy. In September, rumours came that the revival had broken out about Carnarvon and Llanberis slate-quarries. This caused us almost to despair, and ask each other, Can it be possible that God will overlook us, and not respond to our prayers?

"After this we determined to pray more earnestly than ever; and it was not long before we witnessed a new feeling pervading our public meetings, and a few came to join the church. Such was the state of things at Festiniog and Maentwrog before the revival broke out. We were kept suspended between hope and fear till we heard its sound like a mighty wind among the slate-quarries.

"With regard to its character, and the blessed effects it has already produced, I do not know what to say or where to begin. It is singular that the greatest sinners, and the most profligate, were amongst those that were first convinced and converted. When these were present in the means of grace, especially in the prayer-meetings, a sense of awful condemnation, and an agonising dread of God's wrath, seemed to overwhelm them, so that they were forced to cry aloud for mercy. Sometimes they would fall down on their knees, and, one after the other, pray of their own accord for five or ten minutes; others, again, seeing and hearing these, were so deeply affected that there would be nothing done, seen, or heard, but loud sobbing, weeping, and wailing, by all present. Again, perhaps a brother would attempt to pray, but his feelings would soon be so overpowered that he would be obliged to sit down, or rather, as was the case with many, fall down on their faces, to try to suppress their feelings. Sometimes you could hear half-a-dozen pray at the same time, in an under-tone, quite unconscious of each other. It is the broken prayers of the most abandoned characters, confessing their sins and crying for mercy in their simple and childlike language, that affect the people most. I will defy the hardest and the most callous sinner to remain five minutes within hearing of these prayers without being melted into tears. In fact, they are not prayers, but the broken accents and the agonising groans of souls, held, as it were, over the flames of hell. You can easily tell from the character of the prayers whether the petitioner has found peace or not. When the law has done its work with them, and the Saviour found, we might almost say that their prayers are ended; it is then all thanksgiving and praise.

" The blessed result of this revival is astonishing: where there was before much bigotry, bickering, and unpleasant feeling between different parties, there is nothing now but co-operation, love, and zeal, all seeming anxious to rival each other in their efforts to save the *few unconverted* that remain, and who are afraid to come near our religious meetings, lest they should be seized with conviction, and made uneasy about their souls.

" I do not believe that there was a worse place than the village of Maentwrog for its size within the principality. It was notorious for drunkenness and revelry, Sabbath-breaking and swearing, &c. You could hear the school children in passing, when playing together, using the foul language learnt of their parents at home, and that often with oaths and curses; but now these children hold prayer-meetings together. Where there is a group of houses, they assemble at one of them, and hold meetings, at which they read, sing, and pray together, sometimes for hours. Young men, from fifteen to twenty years old, are full of fire; they often meet to pray together in private houses after the public prayer-meeting is over, and continue to pray often till midnight, and sometimes till three and four o'clock in the morning. Women, also, have their prayer-meetings by themselves, and they are as warm in it as the men."

The following letter is from the Rev. R. Killin, incumbent of St David's, Festiniog, dated Feb. 14, 1860 :—

"With much pleasure I comply with your wishes, to give you all the interesting information I can about the wonderful revival with which we have been lately blessed in this favoured locality. I shall confine myself to it, as it bears upon my own congregations, and the general effects upon the community at large, and, therefore, shall say nothing of what took place in the chapels, further than to state, that in its general aspect it is similar in every place of worship in the neighbourhood, and that the work carried on in each contributes to the religious and social welfare of the community.

"In order to give you a correct idea of the work, I must lead you back to the beginning of the year 1859. Hearing at that time of what was taking place in America, South Wales, and Ireland, weekly prayer - meetings were held for the outpouring of the Spirit upon us in this neighbourhood. These have continued to the present time. They have been well attended from the beginning, and a blessing seems to rest upon them. Indeed, a deep feeling seemed to pervade the whole neighbourhood during last winter and the following spring, until the general elections took place in May, which dried up our spirits for a time, though we continued our meetings. On the 7th of September the annual services took place at my church. The effect produced upon the over-crowded congregations assembled together was very solemn and affecting ; many were in tears, being unable to restrain their feelings, and I believe that indelible impressions were made on many a careless soul. Between the 7th of September and the 10th of October, when the revival broke out like a torrent which carries everything before it, the deepest feeling was mani- fested in my congregations ; many were bathed in tears every Sunday, and as many as fifteen persons joined the church as communicants. I ought to have mentioned that prayer-meetings were held in some of the quarries twice a-week, during the dinner hour, last summer and autumn, at one of which, held on the 4th of October, I had the pleasure to assist, accompanied by the rector of Festiniog. The following Sunday was a memorable day here, in many respects. A large open-air prayer-meeting was held in one of the quarries, which deeply affected many.

Some young people broke out rejoicing, in a prayer-meeting held amongst themselves in one of the chapels. There was an unusual solemnity of feeling in church, and some of my people assembled in a cottage afterwards, and held a prayer-meeting, which continued until midnight. The week following will be remembered as long as we live ; three prayer-meetings were held on a mountain, on successive days, at which the quarrymen attended ; and prayer-meetings were held in every place of worship every night in the week, when scores of people joined the different denominations of Christians. From that time to the present, I have not spent more than one evening at home, but have been constantly employed in some religious meeting or other, such as cottage-lectures, communicants'-meetings, prayer-meetings, &c., and you will readily believe that I have enjoyed the season greatly. At first I overworked myself a little, but on the whole, I have been wonderfully supported, both in body and mind.

" During the last five months, about sixty persons have been added to the number of my communicants, many of whom manifest the greatest anxiety for their souls, and have the clearest views of the gospel scheme of salvation. Many of the old communicants are so changed for the better, that they are quite different men from what they were. I never heard such prayers before, although I have been accustomed to prayer-meetings from my early days, under Archdeacon Hughes, of Aberystwith. The earnestness, humility, sense of their own weakness, the clear perception of Christ as their only refuge, and of the Spirit's influence as their support, guide, and consolation, is beyond anything I ever witnessed before. It is very probable that there is much chaff among the wheat now, as well as at other times ; but that there are many sincere Christians among the converts, I have no more doubt than I doubt my own existence. What is most remarkable in them, is their childlike simplicity, their value of the Word of God and prayer, and the preciousness of the Saviour to them ; indeed, I can conscientiously say, that never, since the commencement of my ministry, have I seen men so earnest—they seem to take the kingdom of heaven by force."

The Rev. J. Jones, Independent minister at Maentwrog, corroborates the statements made in the preceding letters. He gives the particulars of a remarkable open-air prayer-meeting, convened by handbill, to which no name was attached, and states that many of the converts date their first serious impressions from that meeting. More than two hundred persons, out of a comparatively small population, have been added to the various churches. Sleepy professors have been thoroughly awakened, many drunkards have become sober, blasphemers now pray, and the self-righteous are seen weeping on account of their sins. Many strange and wonderful things have been wrought ; and the hearers at the various places of worship are become professors of religion, and in their outward conduct give evidence that they are changed in heart by the Spirit of God. Very few indeed remain uninfluenced by this revival. The general character of our village and parish is greatly changed. The majority of the people are now religious.—The letter is concluded with the following statement : " We have many noted examples of prayers offered by parents on behalf of their children, children on behalf of their parents, husbands on behalf of their wives, and wives on behalf of their husbands, being answered. I heard one man saying, with tears in his eyes, that he believed his wife prayed much for him, and that he was saved in answer to her prayers."

Before we leave this portion of the country it may be satisfactory to give extracts from a letter received recently from the Rev. R. Parry, a minister amongst the Calvinistic Methodists at Festiniog :—

"A true revival has taken place here. No power but that of the Holy Ghost could have produced such changes as we see in many persons in this neighbourhood. All classes have, to some extent, partaken of the effects of the revival. The spirits of the old professors are softened thoroughly—they have been brought to a warmer climate, their prayers are more fervent and importunate. The young people who had been brought up religiously from their childhood, have been awakened to see and feel that they are sinners, and to seek the truth in earnest. Hardened sinners have been reclaimed, drunkards made sober, and swearers turned into praying men ; men who were as dark and careless as the brutes, have been brought to seek religion, and are much in prayer. Nothing has caused me so much surprise as to hear these men engage in prayer. They pray so scripturally and earnestly, that I am constrained to believe that they are taught by the Spirit of God. All those who have joined the several churches in this locality, still continue steadfast in their profession. Indeed, I know but very few who have gone back; and, according to present appearances, all are likely to continue faithful unto death. Perhaps we may be disappointed, but we do all in our power to look after them, and lead them to the green pastures. The heavenly fire has not left us yet, and our prayer is that it may remain."

The following communication, respecting the town and neighbourhood of *Bala*, will be read with interest :—

" In a religious sense, Bala is looked upon by the Welsh, and especially by the Calvinistic Methodists, in the same light as the Jews of old regarded Jerusalem. As might be expected, great anxiety was felt by the Lord's people in the place, lest He should leave Bala without that gracious visitation which is enjoyed to such a degree in other places. It appears that for some weeks a deep feeling had possessed the students in the two colleges; * but now that feeling is deepened, a cloud of spiritual gifts and blessings has burst upon them.   Their prayers are like live coals upon the consciences of their hearers, so as to cause the most careless in the town to seek mercy of our Lord Jesus Christ.   There are examples here of the most ungodly brought to feel that there is another world; and if it should please the Lord to bless this visitation to the salvation of their souls, it will be as great a wonder to see them in heaven as to see Manasseh. On a Saturday evening, not long ago, one man went from the prayer-meeting to the public-house. After remaining there for some time, the truth respecting his state as a sinner took hold of his mind so powerfully as to send him out of doors.   On his way home, in the midst of the public street, he began to cry for mercy, and continued doing so for some time after reaching his own house.   The children also have been visited, and their prayers are such as to astonish every one that hears them."

A correspondent says :—" At Bala it is most wonderful. The tutors and students of both colleges have been so blessed with this revival spirit, that they have not done much in the way of study for some time past.   Prayer-meetings have been held, and are still held in every house

* This town has two institutions in which young men are trained for the ministry, one belonging to the Welsh Calvinistic Methodists, under the direction of the Rev. Dr Edwards and the Rev. J. Parry; the other in connexion with the Congregationalists of North Wales, presided over by the Rev. M. Jones.

in Bala, with three or four exceptions; and a friend informed me that they had had some remarkable meetings in the public-houses and inns of the town. It may almost be said that every house is a temple, and every man a priest, offering up a sacrifice to God through Jesus Christ."

The accounts from Merionethshire alone would fill a volume; but without specifying any particulars respecting Dolgelly, Barmouth, Dyffryn, Llandrillo, Corwen, Towyn, and many other places, the whole may be summed up in the words of the Rev. Robert Williams of Aberdovey, in the annual address to the Calvinistic Methodist Churches in this county :—

"Now let me mention a word respecting the revival, its value, and peculiar advantages. It has pleased the Lord during the past year to grant us great things. We are glad that the visitation has been so general in our county. There is scarcely a locality, from Towyn to Gwyddelwern, that has not received, to some extent, the heavenly dew. We find that the addition to the churches of our own denomination is more than FOUR THOUSAND. We venture to say that the last year was an 'acceptable year of the Lord.' In almost every part of our country the hand of God has been stretched out to save those who appeared very far off. To some, like the daughter of Jairus, and the son of the widow of Nain, and Lazarus, it has been a resurrection : resurrection power has made their graves empty for ever."

MONTGOMERYSHIRE.

Although it cannot be said that the awakening is as general in this county as in some others, yet there are districts where " the powers of the world to come" are felt by large multitudes; and ministers of various denominations write with joyful spirits respecting the great enlargement of their churches.

The Rev. J. Williams of *Aberhosan* says :—" I am glad to be able to state that the religion of Jesus continues to attract attention, and has become the topic of conversation in this neighbourhood. ' Great numbers believe and turn to the Lord.' Nearly all the hearers at *Penegos, Aberhosan*, and *Rhydfelin* have become members amongst the various denominations. The prayer-meetings are the principal means of kindling the revival in every place. It was time for the Lord to work. Religion had been set aside. *Literary* and *competition* meetings had turned away the thoughts of the people from the spirituality of Christ's religion."

Later still, the same writer remarks :—" The prayer-meetings had fallen away before the revival ; now they are very popular. We have had prayer-meetings at *Dinas*, as well attended as if the most popular minister in the principality had been announced to preach. Last night, the night of the *fair*, we had a prayer-meeting. The chapel was full, and the streets empty. At this small place about fifty have been added to each of the three denominations, Independents, Calvinistic Methodists, and Wesleyans. A great victory has been gained here. Some of the most unlikely persons have been converted, and they appear to be thoroughly changed. The converts vary in age from ten to eighty. Great things have been done at *Sammah.* Very few of the congregation remain unimpressed. At *Cemmaes* the Calvinistic Methodists have received, as members, nearly the whole of the congregation. I am told that the exceptions are only four or five persons."

At *Llanfair, Newtown*, and various places in the neighbourhood, at *Llanidloes* also, and many smaller places, the

revival gale is felt with more or less power. The following brief extracts will suffice for illustration :—

A correspondent of the *Drysorfa,** writes, as early as
April last :—" I am glad to inform you that the revival
spreads rapidly in these parts (*Machynlleth, Cemmaes,
Dinas-mowddy,* &c.) About thirty have been added to
the church to which I belong within the last fortnight.
Indeed, there are only ten or twelve here who have not
joined us, and even they are wounded deeply. I have
never witnessed anything like that which I now see daily.
You hear of nothing but the revival. Ungodly people
quake and tremble. Those who offer themselves as candidates for church-fellowship weep and mourn, as though
the world were at an end. I have seen a large congregation in this neighbourhood, containing at the time many
scores of hardened, ungodly people, bathed in tears, and as
incapable of leaving the place at the close of the public
service as if their feet had been nailed to the floor of the
chapel. I saw an aged man attempting it, but he failed,
and sat down again. Some of the most ungodly men seemed
to be entirely bewildered ; they could hardly find their
way home that night. Blessed be God ! many of them
found their way to the blood of the Cross. I thank God
I have lived to see the year 1859. God, in His grace, has
done more within the last fortnight in this part of the
country than had been accomplished for an age previously."

A correspondent of the *Baner Cymru* writes, from *Llan-
fyllin,* under date of January 25 :—" A powerful awakening commenced here in a prayer-meeting of young people
connected with the Independents in this town, on the 5th
instant. Many persons who heard the sound of prayer
and praise were attracted to the place. A large congre-

---

* A monthly magazine connected with the Calvinistic Methodists.

gation shortly came together from all parts of the town. Many of the country-people, on their way home from the market, joined us. An old backslider came forward, weeping, and requested an interest in our prayers. A little before midnight the police-officer visited us, and he also caught the revival fire. He spoke to the congregation, and prayed most fervently for himself and all who were present. At this stage of the meeting, a young man lifted up his voice, and in the most pitiful manner entreated that prayer should be offered for his drunken father. It was nearly two o'clock in the morning when the people were induced to separate for their homes. The revival spirit has at length spread amongst all classes, and so strong was the feeling on Sunday evening, that the minister was unable to proceed with his discourse. During the past year there had been a delightful spirit in the church, and upwards of sixty persons were added to us. We had the gentle dew then, but now the cloud has burst upon us, and the great rain has fallen at the commencement of the year 1860. The awakening began at a small chapel, two miles from the town. The various denominations are baptized with the revival spirit. The 9th of January was wholly devoted to prayer. We met in the Town Hall in the morning as one united body, and in the evening in our several places of worship. All the shops and public-houses were closed. Such a day was never seen in this town."

From Llangynog, in another part of the county, we hear, " the revival proceeds with irresistible power. If any one who knew this village a year ago visited it now, he would doubt whether it was really the same place, so great is the change. Those who were celebrated before for their drunkenness, are now equally celebrated for their fervour at the throne of grace. If this work proceeds as it does at present, an irreligious person will not be found amongst us."

The parish of *Llanbrynmair*, also, so long known for its large congregations and active exertions in all that is good, has been favoured with a gracious revival. The Independents and Calvinistic Methodists have had considerable accessions of members. At *Pennant*, in the upper part of the parish, a great and good work has been carried on, and upwards of seventy persons, amongst a thin and scattered population, have made a profession of godliness within a short period. A correspondent at this place says :—" On the western side of Pennant, there is a lead-work called the Conroy Mines. Some of the miners felt a desire to establish an under-ground prayer-meeting, and having made the time and place known, they assembled in considerable numbers. They continued to pray and praise for several hours. Fear and trembling took possession of the most hardened sinners present. This was a remarkable meeting, held in a remarkable place, and conducted by remarkable persons, and it was followed by extraordinary effects. A short time since, some of these people were swearers, blasphemers, and open drunkards—a terror to those around them ; but now we find the same people on their bended knees humbly supplicating forgiveness of sin. 'This is the Lord's doing, and it is marvellous in our eyes.' "

Similar accounts have reached us from many other localities in this county, but as the work in all places is nearly alike in its leading features, the above may suffice.

DENBIGHSHIRE.

From this county joyful tidings are heard. *Denbigh, Ruthin, Llangollen, Llanrwst*, and more than forty other places, report a movement which brings considerable numbers "with weeping and supplication" to "ask the way to Zion, with their faces thitherward."

In the month of October last, a correspondent of the *Baner Cymru* wrote :—"We have the pleasure of stating that the awakening in this place (Denbigh) continues to gather strength. There is nothing in its general features to distinguish it from similar awakenings in other parts of Wales. An idea may be formed of its nature from the fact that it is the topic of conversation amongst all classes, and that its effects are deeply and generally felt throughout the town and neighbourhood. We may look at it in its inner and most spiritual character. The spirit of prayer has been poured out on the Christian churches in this town. The young people were among the first to enjoy it, but it has at length been given to all classes of professors. The revival shews itself in a deep concern for the salvation of souls, in a strong desire to see the Saviour glorified, and in a strong faith in those great and precious promises which relate to these subjects. The character of the prayers offered, and the conversations among the people, are unmistakeable proofs that the Lord works savingly by His Holy Spirit in the souls of the people. There are clear signs of that which the Bible represents as conviction for sin—the pricking of the heart—a broken and contrite spirit—repentance towards God, and faith in our Lord Jesus Christ, in those who offer themselves as candidates for church-membership, and this is very evident in those who were previously immoral in their conduct.

"We may further regard the external circumstances of this movement, and compress the whole into a short compass. The prayer-meetings are very popular. They are attended not only by those who were in the practice of attending the means of grace frequently, but by many who had totally neglected the house of God. There is such a powerful charm in the prayer-meetings, that it is found difficult to terminate them at the usual time ; and although they are held every night, without interruption, they often continue until midnight and even later. It is no uncommon thing to hear persons in the distress of their souls crying out for mercy. Some have experienced very deep convictions. In some cases there have been loud rejoicings in the services. The effects of this movement upon the town are very remarkable. You may observe a general seriousness of manner and deportment. Drunkenness has greatly diminished, and Sabbath desecration is now rare, when compared with former times."

In another communication, bearing a later date, it is said :—" The revival tree continues to take root and to grow in this town. Very many have placed themselves under its shadow, and have tasted its fruits. Converts pour into the churches. The union meetings for prayer are felt to be *a great power.* The chapels are filled to overflowing by multitudes of solemnised people. . . . . The attention of one poor thoughtless sinner was arrested at one of these meetings. He remained in the church meeting at the close of the public service. On his return home, his wife, being struck by his appearance, asked him—'What is the matter?' He replied, 'I am arrested.' She asked, with an oath, 'Who has arrested you?' to which he meekly replied, 'Oh, never swear again ; it is Jesus who has arrested me.' The two wept together."

It is further stated by a Denbigh correspondent :— "Several ungodly characters have been convinced of sin, and whole families have been converted. The following may be given as an example :—A man who was addicted to drinking, and in the practice of going out with his gun on Sundays, told his wife, on his return home on a Sunday evening lately, that he had been in the chapel, and that he had even remained at the church-meeting at the close of the public service. He also said that he much wished she had been there with him. For the first time since their marriage they knelt together in prayer. He slept but little for two nights. He requested his wife to sell the gun, as he should never use it again as he had done, and to use the money to buy a shawl for herself, that she might be able to attend the house of God."

Similar accounts have reached us from *Pentrevoelas, Llansannan, Llangernyw, Pentredwr, Llanrwst,* &c.; but as some of these places will be noticed again in connexion with the results and general effects of the movement, further extracts are not required here.

FLINTSHIRE.

The information received from this county, though not so ample, is nevertheless truly gratifying. The places named as having received showers of blessing are *Holywell, Rhyl, Mostyn, Mold, Rhosesmor, Holt,* and several other localities. A correspondent at Holywell writes in January last:— "We desire to praise Him who dwelleth in the heavens, for the great things we have been permitted to see and feel during the past week. The heavenly fire is kindled in and around this town ; a town which it was feared by many would be the last to receive a visitation from the Spirit of God. Thanks ! the revival has come hither also ! "

After describing the united prayer-meetings held during the second week in January, and on which a special blessing seemed to rest, he adds :—"You may now see in this neighbourhood scores of quarrymen collecting together at the dinner hour to hold prayer-meetings. The heavens are rent by the voice of prayer and praise. On their knees they acknowledge that *they are rocks within rocks.* Drunkenness is diminishing in the town and neighbourhood. The public-houses are emptied, and the people flock to the house of the Lord. It is worthy of remark, that on the 9th of January all the shops were closed, and during the whole of that week business was suspended at half-past six in the evening. The chapels were crowded every evening, even on the evening of the market-day."

The following communication is from *Mostyn*, and dated the 8th of February:—"The three denominations in this place, Calvinistic Methodists, Independents, and Wesleyans, have held united prayer-meetings in their several chapels alternately for some months past, and we have already witnessed some of the blessed effects. During the past week the attendance and interest were such as have never been witnessed before in this district. The effects are seen in the great addition to the Sunday schools, and to the congregations, and to the communion of the various churches. The Bibles and Testaments in the Depository of the Bible Society at this place are in great demand, and are sold rapidly. There is a visible change in the conduct of the colliers, and cursing and swearing have nearly disappeared."

In a recent number of the *Baner Cymru*, a correspondent at *Rhyl* says:—"I rejoice to be able to state that the religious awakening so prevalent in other districts has at length reached this place, and the effects by which it is attended prove it to be a visitation from the Lord. The cause of religion in this place was in a depressed state previously; prayer-meetings were announced, but few attended; the ministry was good, but the sermons preached produced but little effect in inducing the hearers to abandon the ways of sin. The church itself was in a sleepy state."

After giving an interesting account of the united prayer-meetings, the same writer proceeds:—"Other denominations as well as the Calvinistic Methodists partake of this revival. The best possible effects attend it. The young people who had been brought up religiously are now far more earnest. Instead of walking idly about the streets and roads they go to their prayer-meeting. The spirit of prayer seems to be possessed by all classes and ages. Meetings for prayer are separately held by six different parties:—First, by little boys from six to twelve years of age; secondly, by boys from ten to fifteen; thirdly, by young men; fourthly, by girls from eight to fifteen; fifthly, by young women; sixthly, by adults of all ages. The effects are witnessed in the great increase of attendance at the Sunday school. We have never known the Sunday school as large as it is at present. Those who never came to hear the Word are now constant in their attendance at the sanctuary. Many drunkards have been made sober, many who once blasphemed now pray, many of those who mocked and scoffed are now engaged in praising God; and the additions to our church already number upwards of one hundred. When the Almighty works, He adds fresh glory to His cause, fresh beauty surrounds the sanctuary—even the ungodly are compelled to acknowledge there is something greater in religion than the authority and power of man."

CARNARVONSHIRE.

The revival in this county* is so wide-spread in its

* Interesting particulars of the work in some parts of this county may be found in Davies' "Revival in Wales."

extent, and so beneficial in its influence, that a volume of
no small dimensions could be written respecting it.   A
catalogue of the names of the places already favoured with
what is believed to be an outpouring of the Holy Spirit
would of itself be a monument to the praise and glory of
Him who is " the resurrection and the life." Although some
of the churches of various denominations had been moved
in the spring of the year, it was only in the autumn the
movement became so general and powerful that it deservedly
obtained the name by which such extraordinary movements
are generally distinguished.   I have before me the statements of clergymen and ministers of various denominations,
and all unite in adoring gratitude to the Lord, who, after
a season of comparative darkness and deadness, has again
visited His people.   A few extracts will now be given.

The Rev. Mr Griffiths of Bethel writes as follows :—
"The first place in which this wonderful religious movement developed itself in this part of the country is a
populous neighbourhood, about three or four miles east-
ward of Carnarvon, generally called *Waunfawr.*   The
people of God among the Independents and Calvinistic
Methodists were eminently blessed with the 'spirit of grace
and supplications.'   Deep seriousness regarding Divine
things seemed to pervade all minds.   As a consequence
many were turned to the Lord.   Cases of most marvellous
conversions continually took place.   In the course of a
few weeks, about one hundred and twenty new members were added to the Calvinistic Methodists' Church
in the neighbourhood, and upwards of fifty to that of our
own.   A few weeks ago the revival fire broke forth with
marvellous power in the picturesque village of Cwmyglo,
a place not far distant from the Dinorwic slate-quarries.
Soon after this, the whole surrounding country was in a

blaze. Scenes resembling those which occurred on the Day of Pentecost were to be witnessed on every hand. Hundreds were pricked in their heart, and cried out in deep agony, as of old, ' Men and brethren, what shall we do ?' The Lord pours forth His Spirit with an abundance of grace far exceeding our highest expectations. The revival is manifesting itself among all religious denominations, but more especially among the Calvinistic Methodists and Independents, they being the most numerous and influential bodies in this part of the country. A spirit of unity and Christian love has been produced by the revival among the various sections of the Church of Christ, whose effects cannot but tell powerfully on the kingdom of darkness. A spirit of prayer has likewise possessed the Lord's people, which is really wonderful to behold. Our prayer-meetings have become exceedingly popular, and often there is an influence at work which cannot be gainsaid or withstood. The most contrite feelings are made manifest, while some of the most unlikely characters are melted down, and feel constrained to cry aloud for mercy. Our religious meetings now often continue till eleven or twelve o'clock at night, and scores of people retire from them to weep and to pray till the sun of another day dawns upon them. During the silent watches of the night the rocks of our country are to be heard resounding to the voice of prayer and praise, and our majestic mountains testify to the greatness of the work that is being carried on among us. A short time ago, a prayer-meeting for quarrymen was held on one of the mountains between the Dinorwic and Bethesda slate-quarries. About four thousand persons attended, and the Lord graciously met His people. An eye-witness told me it was an occasion to be remembered while memory holds its seat.

"As yet, I am happy to state, there seems to be no abatement of the religious concern thus awakened in our country. It seems rather to advance and spread in all directions. Bethesda and the surrounding neighbourhoods, comprising a most populous and important district, have just caught the sacred flame of revival. A correspondent in the *Welsh Standard*, or *Baner Cymru*, thus refers to the grand movement in this district :—

"'I rejoice in being able to inform your numerous readers that a most powerful revival has just broken out in Bethesda, and the various chapels adjacent thereto. On Saturday, September 3, prayer-meetings were held at two and six o'clock in the evening, and most remarkable meetings they were. God was truly among us. We have felt the Spirit of God at such meetings before; but nothing to what we experienced in these wonderful gatherings. After the meetings had passed away, loud praises were heard in the surrounding fields till midnight—one of the most wonderful things we ever witnessed. Besides the lateness of the hour, it rained heavily; still hundreds of people ran to the place whence issued this unwonted sound. It was found that several of those recently converted had retired to a field in the vicinity of Bethesda, and that, being overpowered by the Spirit of God, they poured out their hearts joyfully before the throne of Divine grace. Some wept; others shouted, "Blessed be the name of God for thus remembering us in mercy." Others cried, "O Lord, save! appear among us as a Saviour to-morrow; an infinite ransom has been found!" Others expressed thanks because God had saved them from the second death. Others, again, repeated some of the most exciting passages of Holy Writ, such as, "Oh that my head were waters, and mine eyes a fountain of tears, that I might weep day and night for the slain of the daughter of my people;" "Oh that they were wise, that they understood this, that they would consider their latter end." Before long, hundreds had assembled there, and the Spirit of God descended upon them in a wondrous manner, till all testified that God really was in that place. In the present movement we have been greatly struck by the fact that so much of the spirit of prayer has possessed the Lord's people. They draw the heaven of heavens, as it were, into every prayer-meeting; hence such congregations as were never before seen are brought together on these occasions. But, in every one of them, there is something more than a large congregation—the prayers penetrate the hearts of those who attend, whether they be male or female, even persons who never scarcely attended a place of worship are impressed; and the fact that people of this description are constrained to cry aloud, and fall down as if dead, proves beyond doubt that this movement is from God, and truly marvellous it is in our sight. I am happy to understand that the revival is breaking out in other places, such as Carneddi, Llanllechid, and all the surrounding neighbourhoods.'

"Three of the churches, under the joint pastoral care of my father and myself, have been signally blessed at this juncture. I have already alluded to the state of things at Waunfawr. The church at Bethel, again, has been wonderfully revived. Upwards of sixty new members have been added thereto in the course of a few weeks. At Shiloh, also, appearances are full of hope; more than twenty new members have been added to the church already."

The Rev. W. Ambrose, of Portmadoc, writes under date of January 25:—"We have had wonderful times here since I wrote to you last. I hope that *hundreds* have been really converted during the last two months. A large number of old, steady, respectable hearers have passed through a wonderful change. I have had the pleasure of seeing some, who were among my *hearers* when I came here, coming forward to make a profession of Christ, after sitting twenty-three years under my ministry. The feeling of that moment I would not exchange for the feeling of an angel in heaven."

The Rev. H. G. Edwards, incumbent of the new church at Llandinorwig, writes on February 13, 1860 :—" Several, I am happy to say, have been added to the church at this place, since the commencement of the revival. It began here in August last, and on the same Sunday night, in different places of worship in the neighbourhood. I do not believe the work has been more real anywhere than in this church, for it came upon us in a manner unsolicited, that is, without any effort on our part to create excitement. It came here like the wind, which ' bloweth where it listeth.' I shall never forget that Sunday night. There was nothing exciting in the subject of my discourse that evening, but the power which accompanied the word was very great, it was a melting power, a power which riveted the attention of every one present. I could see the furthest person in church with his eyes fixed on the preacher. There was no noise, but, on the contrary, great stillness, and every one seemed to be listening for his life, and many were bathed in tears. In a few days after this, about sixteen joined the church at the same meeting. By this time the whole neighbourhood was in a blaze, prayer-meetings were held in the open air, as well as in places of worship, and scores were crying for mercy. The excitement has now subsided, but there is great life here still, and the new converts, with very few exceptions, have thus far remained faithful. There are many who ridicule the revival, but I can bear testimony to its good effects in these parts. The old members have been revived; many moral men, who had been 'halting between two opinions' for many years, have been enabled to 'decide for the Lord,' and some great sinners have been converted.   As far as my own experience goes, I must say I should like to live and die in the blessed atmosphere of the revival."

From the Pennant slate quarries (Bethesda) we hear :— " Strange and wonderful sights are witnessed here.   The chapels are lighted up every night from seven to eight, nine, ten, eleven, and twelve o'clock, and sometimes until one and two in the morning.   A great many persons, from the old man of fourscore to the child of five or six, have power with God and prevail, nor will they let Him go until they are blest.   Truly, this is the greatest outpouring of His Spirit, as a Spirit of life and power, ever experienced by our nation and country.   It is granted to all who use the *key* of fervent prayer, without any exception ; but it would seem that the young people have the largest share, or, being their first love, they shew it more than others.   In them the revival throws its effects far into the future.   At one time our worldliness greatly hindered and injured our heavenly-mindedness ; but now spiritual things absorb the attention, and nothing is heard but religious conversation in going and coming along the roads, in the works, in the shops, and other places.   Ever since the *Queen's visit*, and the dreadful wreck of the *Royal Charter*, religion has been the great topic of the day."

Similar statements are made respecting the work at Pwllhely, Bangor, Carnarvon, Nevin, and the whole of the districts called Lleyn and Eifionydd.   Immense additions are made to the churches.   In one month of the present year it is stated that one hundred and ninety one persons joined the communion of various denominations in the town

of Pwllhely. In the letter communicating this intelligence
it is said:—"The meeting held at the Calvinistic Methodist
Chapel on the night of January 20 was extraordinary.
The sight was awfully stirring—young men who had been
indifferent about their souls before, now cried out the
loudest, 'What must we do to be saved?' while aged men
with hoary hairs were as lively as lambs, praising God for
visiting His people with showers of heavenly rain."

In the month of December last, a correspondent at
Bangor states:—" Although we have no loud expression of
feeling under the ministry, we have amongst us warm hearts
towards the Redeemer and His cause. In one day thirty
persons joined the Calvinistic Methodists at the Tabernacle,
and not a week passes without additions to all denominations in the city. There is a most powerful movement
amongst the children. They meet to pray everywhere, in
the roads, the houses, the school-rooms, &c. They are full
of the spirit of prayer, and it is remarkable what high and
enlarged ideas they have, though expressed in humble
language. They pray for all classes; sometimes a youth
may be heard praying earnestly for an ungodly father, who
was himself a month before a swearer and blasphemer.
We know many examples of the kind. About twenty of
these children have been admitted as candidates at Upper
Bangor."

Later still, it is stated:—" The good work continues to
go on amongst the various congregations in the city and
neighbourhood. Old hearers have been led to decide for
Christ; backsliders are reclaimed; young people who had
been religiously trained, but who had 'sold their birthright,' are now seeking a home in the house of God; prodigals
are returning to their offended Father, and many young

children are under deep religious impressions. . . . We 'rejoice,' but it is 'with trembling.' "

ANGLESEA.

From this small county much information has been sent to the Welsh periodicals and newspapers, and not a few private letters have reached me, some of which have been written with cautious discrimination, but still approving of the work as a whole, and rejoicing in its effects upon the morals of the people.

In November last, a correspondent of the *Baner Cymru* writes :—" The revival in Anglesea continues to spread and to gather strength day by day. Newborough is at present highly favoured. Upwards of one hundred and twenty persons have been added to one church, chiefly young people, but amongst them may be found many a gray-headed sinner, plucked by Divine mercy as brands from the burning. They plead for pardon through the blood of the atonement, with irresistible power. They ' prevail' with God, and often break forth in songs of joy and gladness. At other times it seems as though it rained tears. The prayers of the young converts are most affecting. They pray earnestly for the salvation of others, and more especially for their own relations."

On the 12th of January, the Rev. J. Donne, of Llangefni, writes :—"The revival has reached to all parts of our county, and thousands have been added to the churches. I believe the truly religious element is gaining strength and intensity. *Never* were such things seen in Anglesea. Our church in this place has increased greatly ; we have already received one hundred and forty. This week we have evening prayer-meetings in all the different chapels. We met together in the Town Hall at mid-day, and although this is our market-day, hundreds attended the prayer-meeting."

In December last, a correspondent at *Holyhead* says :— " I am delighted to inform you that the revival, in its full power, has at length reached our town, adding already many hundreds to our churches. It commenced some months ago in the chapel at Kingsland, a small village near the town, and from that time until the present it has gradually increased; and I can venture to say that one-half the *talk* at Holyhead is about the revival, and one-half the thoughts are about God and His wonderful works.

" It is difficult to say when the awakening actually commenced in the town, as additions have been made to the churches week after week for the last year or two. This increase has been very steady and regular amongst the Independents for four years past ; but the first great outward manifestation was on the day when six of the ministers from South Wales paid us a visit, on their return from Ireland. The Independents had set apart a day for preaching the gospel, and these excellent men officiated on the occasion. It was the beginning of a great movement in most of the congregations.

" On Sunday evening two ministers from Cardiganshire preached at the Calvinistic Methodist Chapel. About the middle of one of the sermons a most remarkable effect was produced. The spacious chapel was full, and there was evidently a deep feeling amongst the people. Suddenly the whole assembly moved like a field of corn before the wind, and from many a pent-up heart the suppressed emotions found a vent in loud exclamations ; in some cases it was the voice of terror, and in others of joy."

After a detail of interesting meetings, and of the additions made to the various churches, the writer proceeds :—

" I might tell you of remarkable prayer-meetings, and that in the rocks, woods, and out-houses the voice of prayer and praise is heard at the midnight hour. I might also add that ungodliness, drunkenness, and uncleanness are decreasing in the town, and that a general seriousness has possessed the inhabitants."

A correspondent at *Gaerwen* communicates interesting details respecting the revival work in that and the surrounding districts. Amongst other things, he says :—" On Monday morning, November 28, while the master of the day-school at this place offered up prayer, as was his custom before the school duties commenced, the Lord poured out a ' spirit of grace and supplications' on him, and upon all the children present, about ninety in number, so that they continued in the exercise of prayer and praise until noon. A considerable number of the neighbours assembled to look on and to listen, and they might have said, 'When the Lord turned again the captivity of Zion, we were like them that dream.' They were deeply affected while listening to young children pouring out their full hearts in earnest prayer before the throne of grace. Many of the petitions were remembered and repeated afterwards, and the following may be regarded as a specimen : ' Save me, oh, save me through the blood of Christ. The blood of Jesus can cleanse a great sinner like me.' A little boy prayed for his father with great earnestness, and with weeping eyes, ' Oh, save my father. My father is ungodly, save ; oh, save my father, for Jesus Christ's sake.' Others pleaded for brothers and sisters, and the various members of their families. A woman who came to the place without knowing what was going forward, was so impressed by the sight, that although she had scoffed at every manifestation of feeling in religion only the previous evening, she was so overcome that she joined the children in their devotional exercises."

The same writer adds:—"If I look round the district to *Llanfair, Brynshenkin, Dwyran, Newborough, Bethania, Bethel, Llangristiolus, Llangefni, Gilead,* and including *Gaerwen,* I may say that many hundreds have been added to our churches. In *Newborough* alone we have had two hundred. The Wesleyans and Baptists have had additions. At *Llangefni* the Calvinistic Methodists have had about one hundred fresh members ; and other brethren, the Independents, Wesleyans, and Baptists, have had occasion to rejoice. At *Talwrn,* also, about sixty persons have been added since the 5th of November, the day on which the Rev. D. Morgan, of Yspytty, visited them."

From the north of the island we have similar tidings. A correspondent at Amlwch says:—"A most powerful awakening has been felt in these parts during the last few weeks. It is questionable whether anything more powerful has been felt in America, Ireland, or in any other part of Wales. It has already accomplished great, and almost incredible things. I could compile a volume if I collected together all that is said and done in connexion with this blessed visitation. I am glad to be able to state, that other denominations as well as ourselves (the Calvinistic Methodists) are favoured with this heavenly fire. There is great rejoicing amongst us, and many have joined the Christian Church, and this good work is not likely to end very soon. Thus far it seems to gain in strength, and it has already removed the irreligion of some neighbourhoods. According to present appearances, a drunken man will soon not be found in the town. During the last week the influence of the revival has been very great. We had received one hundred and twenty in the previous weeks, but we have added sixty more this week, making an addition of one hundred and eighty hopeful converts in the town chapel.   At Amlwch Port, eighty; at Nebo, one hundred and seventy; at Silo, eighty; at Bethesda, one hundred and sixty; at Moriah, all the hearers are become members except one or two; and at Bethlehem, ninety persons of all ages have been admitted either as candidates or members."

A correspondent at *Beaumaris* thus writes:—" We have hesitated for some time as to whether we should publish anything respecting the revival in this town, but we have had such unmistakable proofs of a Divine influence that we can now say, ' This is the finger of God.'   The movement commenced amongst the Independents at a church-meeting on Sunday evening about three months ago.   The tabernacle of the congregation was filled with the glory of the Lord, so that every heart was filled with joy, and tears fell like the showers of June through the rays of the sun. It was soon found that the people will not remain in the street to starve in the cold if there is fire on the hearth within.   The tidings of this awakening within the church soon spread throughout the town, and all classes attended the services, expecting still further manifestations of the Spirit's power.   I could never believe that it was possible to raise expectation so rapidly, and it was as marvellous as if ' a nation had been born in a day.'   We have not had any loud rejoicing, but still the feelings were not less powerful, lively, and genuine on that account.   Sinners were converted, being ' pricked in their hearts,' and in receiving them, like the prodigal, into their Father's house, believers had their full cup of joy—they received them as those who had been dead, but were alive again.   All the Dissenting churches of the town received large measures of the Divine influence, and upwards of one hundred and eighty persons have been added to their communion. . . . The hearers have greatly increased, the Sunday schools have nearly doubled their numbers. Many of those who have been for years guilty of Sabbath-breaking, and otherwise living in sin, are now reclaimed—they 'sit at the feet of Jesus clothed and in their right mind.' In those homes where cursing and swearing once were heard, the voice of prayer and praise now ascends to Heaven. It was an affecting sight when a deaf and dumb youth, twenty-two years of age, presented himself at the church-meeting, with his believing parents, to seek the privileges of Christian fellowship. No words could pass between them—they could only look at each other, but in that *look* there were volumes of astonishment, sympathy, and love !"

CHAPTER IV.

AFTER all, the real value of a revival must be estimated by
its moral RESULTS. It becomes us, therefore, to inquire
how far this great and widely-extended religious movement
has benefited the community. More than twelve months
have elapsed since the commencement of the work in
Cardiganshire ; in other places it is of more recent origin,
and every week witnesses a fresh outbreak in new localities,
while in some neighbourhoods the fire is rekindled, and
still larger additions are made to the churches. It may be
too soon to pronounce a judgment—but not too soon to fix
the standard by which alone all revivals are to be estimated,
and to declare, once for all, that in this, as in all other
matters appertaining to life and godliness, our appeal is "to
the law and to the testimony." This is believed and
practised at the present time. On every occasion care is
taken to instruct the people in the *true* and unchangeable
principles of religion. They are cautioned against resting
in a mere outward profession. They are told that excitement is not conversion, that an awakening of the conscience
to a sense of guilt and danger does not always result in a
change of heart. It is strongly and constantly urged that
whatever hope or confidence they may have in their own
minds as to their having "passed from death unto life," it
is a mistake, a delusion, unless it is accompanied by hatred

to sin, and a renunciation of it in every shape and form; love to holiness, and the practical discharge of every moral duty. They are told that the Bible is to ·be the standard of religious feeling, as it is of religious faith. In short, they are admonished to seek a thorough change of heart, and to furnish evidence thereof in holiness of life.

Without exaggeration, and dealing with facts and figures rather than with hopes and desires, a few things may now be stated as *results* of the present revival in the principality.

To *the Church itself*—by which I mean the various religious communities of the land—it has been a season of blessed *awakening*. Under its influence, divisions are healed, old feuds are made up, the "devils" of discord, envy, and strife are "cast out." The temple is cleansed. The spirit of prayer is enjoyed, and in many instances the tongue of the dumb speaks. A higher standard of Christian experience is attained. Many aged disciples feel as though their youth were renewed by the glorious sights they behold, the heavenly music they hear, and the inward joy they experience. No longer in a "strange land" of worldliness and hardness of heart, they have taken down their "harps from the willows"—they sing the Lord's song—they rejoice in Him.

The revival has furnished a *practical demonstration* of the essential *unity* of the Church—the oneness of believers in Christ Jesus. At one time it was thought a great matter if union and co-operation in the simple but holy work of circulating the Bible, without note or comment, could be secured; and when ministers and people of different creeds met in one place and spoke on the same platform, on a subject about which there is hardly room for doubt, it was regarded as a great virtue, and a considerable stretch of Christian liberality! Now, however, in the light and warmth of the revival fire, we look back upon that only as the first step in the path of Christian union—a very small instalment of that love which we owe to our common Saviour, and to His people, as brethren and sisters belonging to the same spiritual family. Amongst the many cheering revival facts may be instanced, the union meetings for prayer, held in churches and chapels, where clergymen and lay-members of the establishment, ministers and office-bearers of the various nonconformist bodies alternately engage in prayer. A clerical correspondent writes thus:—

. . . . "This is the character of our prayer-meetings both at the church and the chapels. Yes, we hold them in the church, and make it indeed the "house of prayer" and praise. There is no school-room here large enough for our union prayer-meetings. Clergymen, preachers, and people, pray together, and God is among us. Where there was much bigotry, bickering, and unpleasant feeling between parties before, and had continued for years, there is nothing now but co-operation, love, and zeal—all appearing anxious to rival each other in their efforts to save the few who remain unconverted, and are afraid to come near the meetings, lest they also should be seized."

A long and deeply-interesting communication has recently appeared in one of the Welsh papers. A translation of one paragraph is subjoined:—

" Last week united meetings for prayer were held in this town. All denominations joined, with the exception of one, which preferred holding separate meetings. The evening meeting on Monday (the 9th of January) was held at R—— chapel. The spacious building was filled to overflowing, with a serious and attentive audience. I have much plea-

sure in stating that the vicar was with us. After reading of
the Scriptures and prayer by one of the brethren, the vicar
ascended the pulpit. It was a delightful sight. He made
some powerful and instructive remarks on the danger of
taking the form of religion, instead of the substance, at a
time like the present; shewing, also, that true religion
would be productive of good fruit. He finished his address
by engaging in prayer. It was solemn and earnest. My
heart leaped for joy in beholding such brotherly union, and
from the depth of my soul I would say, ' Let brotherly love
continue.' "

Another correspondent writes :—" There is one great
stumbling-block removed out of the way—the lack of Christian union. Now the brethren are brought to love one
another with a pure heart fervently. It is just as Christ
commanded. Methodists, Independents, and Wesleyans,
are now united ; and it is evident that the Lord gives His
blessing to us. We are children of one Father, and we are
going to the same eternal home."

Without multiplying instances of this kind, let it suffice
to say that at no former period—no, not even during the
seasons of former religious awakenings—has there been such
a measure of union, such a *fusion*, so to speak, of the various
bodies of Christians. We are led not only to hope, but to
believe that this is *one* of the great objects to be realised
by the present outpouring of the Spirit of the Lord upon
the Churches. An aged Christian, at one of the united
prayer-meetings, stated the fact as it appeared to his own
mind, within his limited sphere of observation, and attri-
buting so great a blessing to Him who is the God of love,
exclaimed, on his bended knees, " O Lord, we thank Thee
that the straw partition, which has so long separated us, is
now on fire ! "

Large *additions* have been made to the churches. Not only have the hearers greatly increased—so much so as to embrace in some instances nearly the entire population—but the number of communicants has more than doubled! It is reported, indeed, that in some neighbourhoods almost all the hearers are become members. In one place in Merionethshire, eight only remained in the class of hearers. In August last I met an elder who had come some miles to invite me to arrange an evening Bible meeting in his neighbourhood, when I should next visit the county of Cardigan—adding, as a reason, that "the men were employed during the day in the lead-mines, and could only attend at night." Knowing that a new place of worship had been recently erected in the vicinity, I said, "How is your new chapel attended?" He replied, coolly, "We have only one hearer now." "How is that?" I asked again with surprise. "Oh!" he said, "all the hearers are in the *society* except one person." By which he meant, that all had either already become members, or been admitted as candidates.

There is an excellent regulation amongst the Calvinistic Methodists of Wales, that no congregation is at liberty (without special permission) to erect a new chapel, or to enlarge an old one, unless it can be done without contracting a debt. Under this law, applications were received from four different places, at the close of last year, for licence to rebuild, or otherwise increase the accommodation, on the plea that "the chapels had become too small to seat the *members* at the communion."

It is impossible to ascertain the exact number of *new* members admitted since the commencement of the revival, a little more than twelve months ago. It is difficult to give even an approximate estimate. I am not aware that a complete list has as yet been prepared, or that any one has hazarded a conjecture on the subject. When I think of the hundreds awakened in single places, and the thousands in separate counties, I am led to conclude, that at least *fifty thousand* persons have taken upon them the yoke of Christ, during the past year, in the principality of Wales.

The only regular report I have seen is the one presented at the assembly of the Welsh Calvinistic Methodists, held at Llangeitho in August last, and this embraced but a single denomination in a single county, (Cardiganshire,) and extended over a period of six months only. It was as follows :—

1859.—From December 31 to June 30.

Received as candidates, ...		6200
Admitted as members, . . .	3595	
The children of members admitted into full communion, ...	1131	
	——	4726
Remaining as candidates, ...		1474

It is probable that similar reports may be made by other denominations. The following parish churches have received a large accession of communicants, but I have not been informed of the exact number—viz. :—Aberystwyth, Llanbadarn-fawr, Llanrhystyd, Aberayron, Tregaron, Tremains, Llanddewi, Ystrad, Trefilan, Silian, Gartheli, Llansaintffraid, Llandilo, Maentwrog, Festiniog, and Blaenau Festiniog.

I have before me the returns from eighty-two places of worship in the county of Merioneth, all belonging to the Calvinistic Methodists, from which I find that the total additions within the year amount to 4048.

From Denbigh a friend writes, February 17, 1860 :—

" The additions to the churches in this town are increasing weekly. They stand thus at present—To the Calvinistic Methodists, 254; Independents, 200; Wesleyans, 100; Baptists, 64—total, 614."

From Aberystwyth, under the same date, the following accessions are reported—" Established Church, about 260; Calvinistic Methodists, 300; Independents, 54; Baptists, 100; Wesleyans, 123; United Wesleyans, 24—total, 871."

A correspondent at Holyhead writes as follows :—" This town has been greatly favoured with an outpouring of the Holy Spirit. The number of converts, up to this time, (January 28,) is as follows—Admitted into the Calvinistic Methodist Churches, 348; Baptists, 332; Independents, 244; Welsh Wesleyans, 195; English Wesleyans, 30— total, 1149."

Bodedern is a small village in the county of Anglesea, and the work there is described thus :—" We have had a revival for about two months. It commenced with the young, whose prayer-meetings are sometimes prolonged to a late hour. Our Christmas-day was spent in prayer to God for the success of His kingdom. During that day seventeen inquirers were received into the church. The number of persons who have joined the various congregations in this village, up to this time, is 178."

It is said of Penrhyn, near Portmadoc, that of the large congregation assembling at one of the chapels, " a few young people only remain in the *world*. Nearly all have joined the church."

From Llanddeiniolen, near Carnarvon, the tidings are equally cheering. I have before me the returns for six weeks only, viz., from September 1 to October 10. During this period there were added to the Calvinistic Methodist churches in the parish, 368; to the Independents, 180; to the Wesleyans, 67; to the Baptists, 40; and to the Episcopal Church, 65—making the total number of fresh communicants, or candidates for communion, 720."

In a communication from Llandegla, in Flintshire, it is stated :—" Many hundreds of persons, and many of them the most ungodly in the neighbourhood, have, within the last fortnight, turned their faces to the various churches. On Sunday, the 25th inst., the outpouring from on high was both powerful and plentiful. When it was published on Sunday evening, at the Calvinistic Methodist Chapel, that a society meeting would be held after the service, all the congregation, with two exceptions, remained; and on the following Tuesday those who did not remain on Sunday applied for admission into the church. Thus all the hearers are become members, or candidates for membership."

The rector of Festiniog states :—" More than three-fourths of our attendants at church, both at Maentwrog and Festiniog, have become communicants. It is the same, if not more so, at St David's Church, in the upper part of the latter parish, and also in all the chapels. We had more than four times as many communicants at the places above named last Christmas than we had twelve months ago."

From *Llanrug*, near Carnarvon, we hear the following tidings :—" More than 140 persons have been added to us in one month, and although the great excitement does not continue, I trust we shall go on increasing."

Without specifying any more instances, it may be stated that, from some hundreds of places not named above, I have information shewing how numerous the converts are —reminding us of that period when it was said of the first preachers of the gospel, and the result of their labours,

" And the hand of the Lord was with them : and a great number believed, and turned unto the Lord." (Acts xi. 21.)

When we speak of numerous additions being made to the churches, it is not to be supposed that all, or even a large proportion, are converts from the ranks of the openly wicked and profane. Very many who had always been hearers of the gospel, with light in their heads, but without grace in their hearts, have now been changed. *Men* who were, upon the whole, moral characters, but who, on account of an occasional outbreak at a fair or a market, were unfit for membership in the Church of Christ; *women*, also, the wives of farmers, tradesmen, and mechanics, of unblemished reputation, willing to give everything, *except themselves*, to the Lord and His cause, are now found amongst the professed followers of Christ. Multitudes of hearers, who had been for a long time " halting between two opinions," have been led to decide for the Lord and His service. Amongst the new members may be found a great number of old *backsliders*, who at one time made a fair profession, and then yielding to temptation, had become more hardened in sin than others, but have now been brought back again with " tears and supplications." It is also encouraging to observe that a large proportion of the awakened are *young people* of both sexes, under twenty years of age. Even *children* may be found amongst the candidates, evidently under a deep concern for their souls. Nor should I omit to state, that in almost every neighbourhood some of the *vilest* and *worst* characters have been reclaimed. Swearers, drunkards, Sabbath-breakers, adulterers, thieves, are found amongst the penitents; and, after a course of instruction and a season of probation, have been admitted into the fellowship of God's people. Some of these characters, in their honest simplicity, are but too ready to confess their sins, and to charge themselves with crimes known only to themselves. An instance of this occurred at a place in Cardiganshire. A man suspected of sheep-stealing, on presenting himself as an inquirer evidently under deep conviction of sin, said, with wild emotion, "I had rather live on potatoes and salt, or bread and water, than steal another sheep." An aged woman, who had led a wretchedly wicked life, but who was now greatly alarmed about her soul, attended a meeting where none but members or candidates were present. It was intimated to her by one of the elders, that as she had only recently felt any anxiety on the subject of religion, it would be better for her to delay her appearance at such meetings for some time longer—a month or thereabouts. She seemed to feel this rebuff most keenly, and replied before all— "God says, *To-day*—the devil says, *To-morrow;* but you put me off for a month." It is needless to add that this poor Magdalen was allowed to remain amongst them as a disciple to be taught, and as a patient to be treated as her sad case required.

On the subject of conversions, a clergyman says :—"I shall give you one or two examples from my own people. In my congregation for several years was a young man, who had of late years become very dissipated. His father had been a communicant with me for many years, and latterly, as he told me himself, had been praying much for his own son, who was on the high road to ruin. The visit of the Rev. D. Howell, of Swansea, to the neighbourhood in September last, made a deep impression upon him, and he joined my communicants' meeting on the 9th of October, and took part in a prayer-meeting held by those who had lately joined the church ; but what a prayer it was ! His confession of his former sins was such, that it melted into tears all who heard him; and then his pleading the promises of God to keep him, through His almighty power, was most touching. Ever since, prayer is his delight. For months together, he never missed one meeting, though held every night in the week, and two or three successively on the same evening. Often has he been in out-houses, or on the mountain, praying until midnight, during the cold winter nights. In going from his home to the quarry one day, he was compelled to turn out of his path three times, to pray behind some cliffs, although his house is only half a mile from the quarry. The fact is, he lives in prayer. You will again see his value of the Bible from the following conversation which I had with him and others. I observed that the Word of God was the daily food of the spiritual man. One of them replied, he did not think any one now neglected reading the Bible; another said, he read one chapter every morning, even when he had slept late! but the young man above referred to said, he could not leave off until he had read three or four chapters. He is learning the Epistle to the Hebrews by heart, and often stays up until twelve or one o'clock in the morning learning it, after the family have retired to rest, that he may have quiet in the kitchen, which is the only room he can have in the house. Emphatically, he might be called a Bible Christian, whose very breath is prayer. Occasionally I find him in the greatest distress, walking in darkness. One evening he told me, " I do believe the Lord has now left me;" but, generally, he rejoices in the full assurance of his salvation. There are several of the new converts similar to this young man.

A few more cases of conversion are now added :—" A brother who had spent the whole night in prayer returned home, and found his wife, who was unconverted, in a very angry mood, and was chiding him rather severely. He, however, fell upon his knees, saying, ' O God, help me to pray once more.' He continued to supplicate the throne of Divine grace till his companion in life also loudly cried for mercy. On the evening of the same day she joined the company of the faithful.

" A man had been treated with ardent spirits by some evil-disposed persons, with a view to create a disturbance, and thus to injure the revival movement. Instead of this he went home, and, as he passed by the minister's house, he began to cry aloud for mercy. The arrow of conviction had pierced his heart. He called there again next morning, overwhelmed with a sense of his lost condition; and on the following night he became a candidate for church membership.

" Before the cold weather set in, there were many who spent whole nights out, praying by themselves along the mountains, and other places. Some of my own people used to do so, and they told me of it.

" On one such occasion the following incident occurred :—

" One night ——'s gamekeeper, being out on his beat on the mountain above ——, heard a noise on the other side of a stone wall, and having listened, he found it was a poor sinner confessing his sins, and praying to God. It affected the keeper so much, that he left quietly, and felt much concern about his own soul. That gamekeeper is now a member of my church, and one of the most gifted in prayer of all the new converts that we have had."

The general establishment of *family worship* is another blessed result of the present awakening. This is expected from all the converts, and they set about it forthwith.

They are told that they must not rest satisfied with prayer and praise in the public sanctuary, but that God must be worshipped in their own houses by their assembled families; and, as in the case of Abraham, Jehovah must have an altar in their dwelling. Inability and timidity are not admitted as excuses. They must *try*. Reading a chapter is comparatively easy, and as "prayer is the soul's sincere desire," to be expressed in "the simplest form of speech," they are encouraged to make the effort; to do it immediately, in the ardour of "first love." Nor is the admonition limited to the heads of families—it is addressed to the children, and even the servants. If the husband, the father, the master, does not choose to set up an altar under the domestic roof, then if he has a wife, a child, or a servant who fears God, he is solicited to allow one of them to conduct the worship of the household, morning and evening. It is delightful to contemplate the spectacle presented in many of the villages, and some of the smaller towns, where, in the *majority* of the dwellings, the voice of prayer is heard, not unfrequently accompanied by a hymn of praise. In many of these dwellings the chapter is not always read, or the prayer offered by the head of the family, who is, and ought to be, the prophet and priest, as well as king in his own house, but all the professing members of the family take the "duty" in turns. In some instances the piety of a single member of the family has produced an impression upon the rest, and such an impression as has led to the happiest results. We are told of a family consisting of a father and mother and two children. The son, aged twelve, was the first to be awakened. He entered the *society* as a candidate, and at one of the church-meetings the duty and privilege of family worship was urged on the new converts. John heard it, and applied it to himself. On his return home, he told his mother that, if it was agreeable to her and to his father, he should like to read and pray every morning and evening. The mother mentioned this to her husband, who discouraged the idea. "The boy," said he, "does not know what he is about; let him alone for a little while, and the desire will cease." John, however, asked again, and continued to ask, until at length permission was granted. After supper, one night, the Bible was opened, and John read the chapter very courageously. This being done, all knelt down together for the first time; but not a word could the poor boy utter. A long and painful pause ensued. At length the sister, unable to restrain herself any longer, tittered aloud; and upon this John brought forth his first petition—"O Lord, give grace to my sister Mary." His lips once opened, he was able to proceed, and in broken accents he poured out his soul in supplications for himself and all around him. An impression was made; the daily cares of the house and the farm could not efface it. The next time John went to the church-meeting, his mother said, "I will go with you;" and when she mentioned her intention to her husband, he replied, "I will go too." When Mary was informed that all three intended going to chapel, and that she was to take care of the house during their absence, she exclaimed with tears, "You shall not go without me!" Thus the piety and example of one, and he the youngest in the family, became the means, under God, of awakening a concern in the minds of all. The father at length was able to say, "As for me and my house, we will serve the Lord."

The revival has given a powerful impulse to the cause of *temperance*. The Welsh are not supposed to be more addicted to drunkenness than the English, Scotch, or Irish, and yet it must be acknowledged that in the towns, and even in the villages, more especially in the iron and coal districts, a vast amount of intemperance existed. Notwithstanding the great efforts made in times past to stem the torrent by means of "temperance," and "total abstinence" societies, drunkenness continued to an alarming extent. Even where the drinking did not end in absolute intoxication, the habit of *tippling* was deep-rooted and wide-spread, and this, with the generally attendant habit of smoking, absorbed a vast amount of the earnings of the artisan and the labourer; thereby bringing distress and poverty upon themselves and their unhappy families. And even professedly religious people were too often found amongst the frequenters of public-houses. Drinking had become a snare to young men, who at one time promised well; and very many attribute their backsliding to the indulgence of drinking habits. Multitudes who had taken the "*pledge*" of total abstinence had fallen back again into their former courses, and their end was likely to be worse than their beginning. It was at this juncture that the revival broke forth;—at the time when godly people feared that the tide of intemperance, instead of ebbing, was flowing in more rapidly, another agency was raised up to arrest its progress. Although total abstinence is not made a condition of membership in any church, it is strongly recommended to the new candidates, whether young or old, both as a safeguard to themselves and as an example to others. It is thought that most of the men and youths who have been admitted as members amongst the Calvinistic Methodists have voluntarily taken the "pledge;" and it is hoped that having "vowed," they will be enabled conscientiously and perseveringly to "pay their vows to the Lord."

We cannot wonder, therefore, that the consumption of

ale and spirits should diminish in many districts ; nor are we surprised when we hear that public-houses are closed. The landlady of a road-side inn gave a very satisfactory reason for taking down the sign, and for countermanding the order for Bristol porter—it was " that she had only drawn three half-pints in a month !" The receipts at one place are said to have been reduced from ten pounds in the week to ten shillings. We are told that in another place a man had brewed a quantity of beer for sale at the approaching fair ; but between the brewing and the fair, the revival influence interposed—he became uneasy about his soul, and being troubled about the lawfulness of selling beer to others, he actually poured the contents of his casks into the river Tivy !

In another revival district, the landlord of a public-house became so concerned about his own soul that his business became exceedingly disagreeable to him. He could not reconcile it with his conscience to sell intoxicating drinks any longer, and to allow his house to become the scene of riot and dissipation. Having resolved to give up the business, he took down his signboard, and on a given night invited the minister and the people to hold a prayer-meeting in his house with a view to consecrate it to other purposes. It was a season of great interest and rejoicing.

It is said that at and near *Bethesda*, in Carnarvonshire, about twelve public-houses have been closed, partly on account of the change in the views of the parties who held them, and partly because the hope of gain from this quarter had quite disappeared.

From another locality it is reported :—" Public-houses which used to be frequented by young men from the quarries, and others, have nearly become empty." Another says :— " The effect the revival has had on the community at large is wonderful. Drunkenness has all but disappeared for some time past. The inhabitants of my district are about two thousand, but we have only two public-houses, and they have had scarcely any business done in them during the winter." Mr Gee, of Denbigh, writes, on February 13, 1860 :—" Drunkenness is scarcely known in the neighbourhood; so much has it decreased that the Mayor of Denbigh has not had a case before him since the 9th of November, except one—and he was a ' tramp,' an entire stranger to the town."

A correspondent from the neighbourhood of Carnarvon says :—" There is not only less drinking than usual, but fewer public-houses—two have been closed at Ebenezer and Clwt-y-bont. A trial of the effects of the revival on the young men of the quarries was made in the last winter fair at Carnarvon. They generally took the lead in drunkenness and dissipation, but how different the scene last time ! Instead of spending their time in the taverns drinking and feasting, they held meetings to pray for the salvation of sinners and to praise God for their own conversion. A prayer-meeting, long to be remembered, was held at *Pendref* chapel on the fair night, and another on the second day of the fair at *Moriah* chapel, at two o'clock in the afternoon. The fair throughout was such as had never been seen before. The public-houses were nearly empty, and all appeared to attend to their proper business. Some one was asked, ' What kind of fair have you had this year ?' The reply was, ' The people called for something to eat as usual, but there was very little drinking.' On their return home, the young people testified how much more happy they were now when able to go and return from the fair, without following the usual practice of drinking to excess. It was only twelve months before, that many of them had been guilty of drinking, quarrelling, and fighting. Now, for the first time, they had found that the way of duty is the way of pleasure and safety."

A correspondent from Yspytty says :—"We are about to make another attack on the ungodly world, and resolve in the strength of the Lord to persevere and to conquer until there shall not be within our district a single ungodly person. We hope to see the day when 'Holiness unto the Lord' shall be written over the public-houses, instead of the 'Lion,' the 'Bear,' &c., &c. They have already been the target for our arrows. They are nearly empty from morning until evening, and the landlords are beginning to complain. One of them remarked lately in conversation, 'This revival occasions me a great loss.' 'Oh,' said another, 'this will soon pass away.' 'What will that avail,' was the reply, 'when I now lose twelve pounds every month.' A land-lady once went to the Rev. D. Morgan to ask why he had warned the people against coming to her house since she had a regular licence from the Government. She was, however, soon silenced, and even brought to acknowledge that the traffic in drink was to come to an end."

We may add to these results a few cases of *individual conversions :*—

The Rev. Griffith Davies, of Aberystwyth, communicates the following facts:—"At a prayer-meeting held in the Sunday school-room, Skinner Street, in this town, a man engaged in prayer, who had been, previous to his conversion, one of the most notoriously wicked characters in the town. The entire congregation was moved by this prayer, and the feelings of all were greatly excited. Suddenly, a man was heard exclaiming, 'What is the matter with me?' and in an instant he fell to the ground. It seemed as if he had been prostrated by a sun-stroke. The fall of the persecutor of Tarsus could scarcely have been more sudden. This man was a most abandoned, openly-profane sinner, a drunkard, swearer, and cruel husband. He was also an infidel in opinion as well as in practice. He was, nevertheless, an intelligent man, beyond most of his own class. It is to be remarked that he had been for years the chief companion of the man who had engaged in prayer at this meeting. Behold, then, the blasphemer, the sceptic, the drunkard, convinced of his sins while listening to the prayer of his former companion in wickedness! He has been ever since *another* man, and I believe I may say a *new* man. He is the reverse of everything he was before. For some weeks he appeared as if he would lose his reason, in consequence of the strength of his convictions, but at length he found salvation in Christ, whose blood cleanseth from all sin.

"Many of the recent converts furnish strong evidence of the reality of the change which they profess to have experienced. There is in this town a person who had led a most ungodly life, but during this revival he has been brought to feel himself a sinner, and to trust in Christ as his only Saviour. He is as remarkable for his zeal in religion as he was formerly in the service of Satan. He works in the foundry. In order to try him to the utmost, one of his fellow-workmen commenced a series of provocations. He struck him with his fist. All he said in reply was, 'Don't.' He again pushed him against a piece of iron, which caused him great suffering. To this he only said, 'Don't act foolishly.' If he had received such provocations six months before, he would have retaliated with fearful vengeance, but he was now taught of Him who was 'meek and lowly in heart'—and like Him, 'when he was reviled, he reviled not again, and when he suffered, he threatened not.'

" I have known several examples of conversion in answer to prayer. In the neighbourhood of B. there lived a young man who had been very ungodly, but who, after his own conversion, was very anxious for the salvation of his sister. At the close of the Sunday school he prayed specially for his own beloved sister. She seemed indifferent and hardened, and instead of going to the chapel or to the school, she cast herself on her bed, and was fast asleep at the time when her brother prayed for her. She said afterwards that in her sleep she dreamed that her brother was praying for her at the time. This dream made an impression upon her. She became serious, and at the service of that evening she was further impressed, and to such a degree that, like her brother, she is now an humble but zealous follower of the Lord Jesus."

The following facts are from the pen of the Rev. Thomas Rees of Beaufort:—"The Congregational, and the Calvinistic Methodist Churches at Ebbw-vale, in this county, are blessed with a large measure of Divine influence. At a prayer-meeting in the Independent chapel, on Monday evening the 12th instant, the attendance being unusually large, a person, who had been a member of the church for nearly twenty years, was requested to engage in prayer. Having uttered a few sentences, he began to pray for the conversion of his aged father in a most pathetic manner. His feelings soon overpowered him, and in an instant the whole congregation were so affected, that they sobbed aloud. When the excitement had in some measure subsided, the minister requested those of the hearers who had a desire to join the church, to remain behind. Thirteen did so, and amongst them was the father of this man. The gray-headed sinner came weeping to the communion-table to be spoken to.

"Some time ago, in the neighbourhood of Swansea, a

dissolute young man, the eldest son of a widow, was one Sabbath evening on the road-side, waiting for his wicked companions. A good man on his way to chapel invited him to go with him to the house of God, which he very reluctantly did, and it pleased the Lord by His Spirit to touch his heart. His mother was surprised to see him returning home so early, but in a few minutes a younger brother remarked, 'We have had a strange meeting to-night. Every one was weeping there, and my brother Daniel wept also.' We will not attempt to describe the feelings of the mother on hearing of so marvellous and unexpected a change in her wild and undutiful son. The young man has since that period led a new life.

"Scarcely any physical prostrations occur, but the intense feeling manifested is often remarkable. Last Sabbath evening, at Libanus chapel, near Brecon, those of the congregation who were affected were invited to stay after the close of the public service with the members. At a late hour the chapel-keeper, when locking the doors, overheard a person groaning in the adjoining grave-yard. He went in, and to his surprise found a young man there in the greatest mental agony. It appears that he was too timid to remain with the candidates in the chapel, and too much affected to go home.

"Two men were lately returning home from a beer-shop at a very late hour. One of them said to the other, 'When I get into the house to-night my wife will scold me dreadfully.' 'Oh,' said his companion, 'I shall have something ten times more intolerable than scolding. My wife is always quiet, but she weeps and speaks to me about my soul ; and her words are burning like fire in my conscience.' Having reached his house, his wife, as he expected, met him at the door, weeping. He retired to his

bed immediately and slept, but his pious wife could not
sleep. She wrestled with her God for hours on his behalf.
About three o'clock in the morning he awoke, and saw her
standing at the bed-side, and wetting his face and pillow
with her warm tears. 'Margaret,' said he, 'what is the
matter with you?' She replied, 'The thought that my
dear husband is an enemy to my beloved Saviour, and that
he is likely to have his eternal portion with damned spirits,
almost breaks my heart.' This was too much for him; he
rose and knelt by his wife, and prayed for mercy. They
are now a happy couple, rejoicing in the hope of dwelling
together for ever in heaven.

"At a village in North Wales there was a young man,
who, though young, had become so hardened as to laugh
at the tears and prayers of his pious mother. One evening
in the first week of last month, he stood outside the win-
dows of the village chapel to mock the good people who
were holding a prayer-meeting there. An elderly woman
seeing him, rebuked him, but his insolent reply was, 'Go
you and serve your Master, and let me alone to serve
mine.' A few minutes after he was found lying in the
road, with his face to the ground. A person happening to
pass raised him up, and having recognised him, inquired
what ailed him. 'I do not know,' said he, 'unless God
is about to kill me; I am very ill.' His sickness, however, was 'not unto death,' but for the glory of God. He
was taken home and laid on the bed. For some days he
suffered the most dreadful mental agony, but at length
found peace in believing; and this mocker is now one of
the most earnest men of prayer in the village."

The Rev. Mr Griffith, in communicating information respecting the awakening at Llanrug and Cwm-y-Glo, states
the following facts :—

" The drunkards, swearers, and Sabbath-breakers are now seeking pardon from that merciful God whom they have offended, and are endeavouring to flee from the wrath to come. One hardened young man, who often got drunk, said to some of his companions that this wonderful work would not cause him to forsake his evil ways; but in less than half-an-hour he was seized with a feeling that caused him to cry out for mercy, or he would eternally perish. He is now amongst them a sinner saved through grace. Another young man said he would get something to drink, so as to be fit to persecute those of his acquaintances that he knew were assembled there. He approached the place and shouted, ' I am Saul of Tarsus coming to persecute you, lads ;' but before he left the place he became sober enough, and began to cry for mercy, and was laid low at the foot of the Cross."

CHAPTER V.

" IF the revival now in the country is of God, it will be
followed by such effects as will prove it such ; the public-
houses will become less numerous than our chapels ; the
debts remaining on our places of worship will be wiped
away ; and day-schools will be established to instruct the
ignorant.   In a word, if it is a religious revival, it will also
be a social revival."   Such were the words of an eminent
Welsh minister, on a very public occasion, when preaching
in the presence of many thousands of hearers, and amongst
them some hundreds of ministers, elders, and deacons.   In
a recent number of a Welsh newspaper, there is an excellent
letter from a clergyman, in which he says, " What is the
revival ?   Repentance for sin, faith in the only Saviour,
peace with God, joy in the Holy Ghost, and newness of
life.   These are its peculiar characteristics.   Some imper-
fections may be found in connexion with it ; but they are
not of much importance when compared with its good
effects.   Who, that knows anything of true religion, will
deny, that the revival in Ireland and in Wales, is the
work of God !"

The Great Teacher has said, " By their fruits ye shall
know them ; shall men gather figs from thorns, or grapes
from thistles ?   The good tree will bring forth good fruit ;"
and we can only judge of the character of this marvellous

movement by the effect it produces on the hearts, lives, and general habits of those who profess to feel its influence.

A selection will now be made from a mass of correspondence, with a view to illustrate this subject.

Cardiganshire.—The Rev. W. Herbert, Vicar of *Llansaintffraid*, speaks of the revival thus :—" The additions to my church during the past year consists of one hundred and fifteen members. In this locality the movement was not noisy, but calm, silent, and sober. The good effects which, I am happy to say, are still visible, are these—the Sabbath is more strictly observed, the house of God is better attended, family prayer is set up in many houses where nothing but cursing and swearing were heard before, drunkards are become sober, &c. These are the good effects of the revival in this place."

Another clergyman in the same neighbourhood says :—" The increase of members at my church has been about forty to fifty—all young people. May God preserve them by His grace, and keep them to eternal life ! Though I dread the future, yet my consolation is, that He who gave the grace will continue it, and that ' He who hath begun a good work will finish it until the day of Jesus Christ.' There is already a very evident improvement in the morals of the people. Twelve months ago there were no less than twenty public-houses in this small place, well supported. The people were addicted to drinking, and exhibited a contemptuous dislike of everything and everbody around them, so that I had almost abandoned the place in despair to everything that was vile and vicious. But mark the change. I came here on the day when Colonel Powell made his first appearance after his election, and although beer was given freely at every public-house, I only saw one solitary instance of drunkenness throughout the day, and that was a poor half-witted beggar."

Goginan Lead Mines, near Aberystwyth.—"The practice of the miners formerly was to meet together to smoke, and to talk of things which will not bear repetition; but now there is a change. Prayer-meetings are held daily, even in the mines, far below the surface of the earth, and it is evident that the God of heaven smiles upon them. The clefts of the rocks in which they assemble for prayer and praise, serve to remind them of the cleft in another rock, even Christ, in which the sinner is permitted to behold the Divine glory. There is only one person working in this mine who is not a professor of religion, and his conversion is made a subject of fervent prayer."

Llanddeiniol.—"The people of this place appear very solemn at the present time. The young people, instead of meeting at the cross-roads to relate foolish and superstitious stories, now assemble in the house of God for the purpose of prayer, and on many occasions the Divine influences are overpowering. The most thoughtless and inconsiderate are now amongst the praying people, and it is enough to melt the hardest heart to hear these men crying out for pardon through the blood of Christ." . . . .

Aberystwyth.—"It is a rare thing to see a drunken man passing through the turnpike gates on a market or fair day. The Gogerddan races, generally attended by thousands, were this year only witnessed by hundreds. It was but a small affair when compared with former years. Strangers from England were the leading characters, joined by some of the gentry of the neighbourhood. The 'common people' have found better employment; and they pray heartily for those who still support that which occasions so much sin and wickedness."

Frongoch Lead Mines, near Aberystwyth.—Captain Collins writes, March 20 1860 :—"About eleven years ago I left Cornwall, and came to this place as agent in the mine-works. I found the majority of the workmen living in sin—Sabbath-breaking and drunkenness prevailed to a most alarming extent. We pay the men on Saturday, once in the month. On the Monday following, many of them used to come to their work with bruised faces and blackened eyes ; some would remain in the public-houses for two or three days, and even a week, where they spent a great portion of their hard earnings, leaving their families destitute of the common necessaries of life. On this account we felt compelled to impose a fine for neglect of work, and when other means did not succeed, to discharge them altogether.

"But about two years since, the churches became more earnest in prayer. God heard and answered. He poured out His Holy Spirit. Sabbath-breakers and drunkards were convinced of sin, and began to cry out for mercy. They obtained it, and were comforted. The change which has taken place is beyond everything I have ever known. I have seen great revivals in Cornwall, but nothing to be compared with the present awakening in these parts. I believe there is not a drunkard, or Sabbath-breaker, or openly immoral person to be found amongst our two hundred workmen. The men work in *pairs*, or *companies* of four, six, eight, twelve, twenty, more or less. There is not a company, small or large, without its prayer-meeting, held under-ground previous to the commencement of work. The meetings are conducted in the usual way, but shorter. They are allowed fifteen or twenty minutes to get into their places—and this time they formerly spent in telling stories, often *lies*, and in doing that which did not profit them. But now this interval is spent in prayer. The singing is admirable.　It is delightful to hear the voice of praise ascending to Heaven from the very depths of the earth! The men work for three or four hours, and then they sit down to their refreshments.　One of the company asks a blessing, and when they have finished their meal, they return thanks, and resume their work.　At the end of the week, as many as can make it convenient meet together in the most suitable spot under-ground to join in thanksgiving and praise for the mercies of the past week.

" The *surface people*, namely, the boys and girls employed on the *flooring*, have an hour allowed for dinner, and these, during the summer season, get into one of the machine houses to spend half-an-hour in prayer and praise.　It is truly affecting to see fifty or sixty young people on their knees in the attitude of prayer!　The 12th of July was a day of thanksgiving and prayer.　The meeting was held on the top of the mountain near the mines, and was attended by nearly three thousand people.　It was conducted in Welsh and English—Churchmen, Calvinistic Methodists, Wesleyans, and Baptists took part in it.　We had prayers, hymns, and short addresses, and while memory holds its seat, I shall never forget this meeting.　We hope, God willing, to have another meeting of the same kind in July next.　There is hardly a house in the whole neighbourhood without a family altar."

Nantglyn.—" Here many old backsliders have returned to the house of God, and those we had long expected to take upon them the yoke of Christ, have been brought to a decision.　The hearers have greatly increased, and the Sunday school is more numerously attended.　Those who at first railed at the revival, are now silenced.　There is a wide-spread religious feeling in the neighbourhood."—*January* 1860.

Llangernyw.—" Religion and its concerns are the chief topics of conversation throughout the neighbourhood. Drunkenness is diminishing, and other sins seem to die away. The very countenances of the young people seem changed—the proud are in the dust—the frivolous are sober-minded—those who never attended the sanctuary now attend the prayer-meetings. There is a visible change in the converts—many of them weep almost constantly— are hardly able to sleep at night. Women may be seen with the open Bible on their tables at home, and before they have peace in believing, they are in great agitation and concern. They are brought to the dust, and learn that this is the way to heaven."—*January,* 1860.

Barmouth.—" The young people of our town are wonder- fully changed. A few months ago they would have treated any advice given them with indifference, but now there are scores who seek life in the death of Christ."—*December* 1859.

Festiniog (Bethesda.)—" The wilderness has become a paradise. The converts, by the holiness of their lives, write the history of the revival with a pen of iron and of lead."— *November* 1859.

Dolgelley.—" Three months have passed since the awak- ening commenced in this town. It is natural to ask, Are there any good fruits? has it produced an effect on the morals of the place? are there fewer drunkards seen in the streets? and is there less Sabbath desecration? These are the things to be expected as the fruits of a religious revival, and we believe that such have been its effects in this town. The idlers, who formerly met at the corners of the streets to gossip, now spend their evenings at the prayer-meetings. Those wanderers who delighted in walking about on the Lord's-day, now hear the gospel every Sabbath-day with devout attention, and seem as if they were determined to devote the remainder of their lives to the service and glory of Him whom they formerly blasphemed. The public-houses close earlier, and are less frequented than formerly. The small beer-houses, formerly filled on Saturday nights by the very worst and vilest of the population, and where it was necessary to procure the aid of the police to keep order, are now nearly empty, and are closed by ten o'clock. The number of drunken persons brought before the magistrates has greatly diminished. In the three months commencing October 26 1858, twelve were fined " five shillings and costs" for drunkenness and unruly conduct in the town of Dolgelley, and all living in the town except one. Two were fined for an assault on the police in a state of drunkenness. But in the three months commencing on the same day in October last, only two persons were brought before the magistrates for any offence occasioned by drunkenness, and one of these was a stranger to the place. This fact proves that intemperance has decreased in the town. Indeed, the inhabitants are greatly altered in their morals and habits within the last nine months ; and to what are we to attribute this change for the better, if not to the revival ? We had at one time a flourishing total abstinence society, but the drinking continued nevertheless, and drunkards were seen everywhere. We had an excellent literary institution, but the young people preferred wasting their precious time in the streets rather than engage in the pursuit of knowledge. But at length the *revival* came, — it cleared the public-houses, swept the streets, and brought the wanderers to the means of grace. The revival has given ample evidence that it is of God, by its beneficial effects upon men on whom nothing could produce an impression before. It has been the means of uniting the various religious bodies in closer bonds than ever. They no longer look *shy* at those who do not belong to their own party. To win sinners to Christ is the aim of all. They behold each other with cheerful countenances, and pray for the prosperity of all alike. They belong to one family—they are brethren—and have one common Saviour."—*February* 1860.

Llanddeiniolen, near Carnarvon.—" The good effects of the revival may be seen on the entire neighbourhood, as well as upon those who have made a formal profession of religion. There is a general change throughout the *quarries*. The cursing and swearing, with the light and profane conversations, have ceased ; we have prayer-meetings instead, and seriousness is stamped on every countenance. The most thoughtless are ready to acknowledge that something extraordinary has taken place, and one has said, that 'the days of earth are now like the days of heaven.' Not only is there less drinking, but the public-houses are decreasing in number ; two have been closed lately at Ebenezer and Clwt-y-bont.

" The effects of the awakening were seen at the last winter fair at Carnarvon. The quarrymen were generally the leaders in drunkenness ; but the change witnessed during the last fair was very great. Instead of spending their time in the taverns, they had prayer-meetings, in which they sought the salvation of others, and praised the Lord for their own conversion. On the first night of the fair, a prayer-meeting, that will long be remembered, was held at *Pendref* chapel, and another, at two o'clock the second fair day, at *Moriah*. The fair throughout was such as had not been seen within the memory of man. The public-houses were comparatively empty, and all seemed to be intent on their proper business. A landlord's daughter was asked,

'What kind of fair have you had?' To which she replied,
'We have had very good eating, but *very little drinking.*'"—
December 1859.

Llanberis.—"From the commencement of the revival
until the present time, we have had an addition of ninety
persons, most of whom are young people who have spent
their days in idleness, drunkenness, swearing, taking the
Lord's name in vain—and were as unconcerned about religion and their souls as the brute beasts. Within the last
few years, we found a generation of hardened young people
springing up among us, totally devoid of the fear of God.
But by this time, the young people are thoroughly hum-
bled—easily entreated—kind—and very liberal in their
contributions towards the Redeemer's cause."—*October*
1859.

Llanllechid.—"Since the commencement of the revival
among us, the neighbourhood presents a new aspect. It
may be said that we have a 'new heaven' in the chapel,
and a 'new earth' in the roads and the fields. Instead of
prowling about the neighbourhood at night, the young men
now assemble in the various places of worship to pray. Instead of the oaths and obscene language formerly used in
every direction, we now hear the voice of praise all around.
The annual fair at this place was very different this year.
Formerly the young people attended in crowds at the close
of the day, but this year there was hardly anything worth
calling a fair. Prayer-meetings were held in the chapel at
two in the afternoon, and again at seven in the evening."—
November 1859.

Penmachno.—"We are glad to be able to state that the
spirit of the present revival has made its appearance in a
body of good works,—such as brotherly love, alms to the
poor, visiting the sick, prayer for those who are still unsaved,

doing good to all—and thus shew that we are not angry with men, but with their sins."—*October* 1859.

Llansannan.—"There are but few in this neighbourhood who have not, in some degree, felt the powerful operations of the Spirit of God upon their minds. Those who once served Satan with all their might have surrendered the weapons of rebellion, and have sought a place in the Lord's house. It is delightful to see the young people, who were formerly in the bondage of sin, now under the yoke of Christ, and learning of Him who is meek and lowly in heart. The wildest sinners are turned. All things are possible with God."—*March* 1860.

Bangor, Bethesda, &c.—"Before this gracious visitation, the moral state of this neighbourhood was most deplorable. The young people, especially, appeared to grow worse and worse, shaking off every religious restraint, becoming more callous and thoughtless, and acting as though they thought that religion was a barrier to mental vigour and progress. The openly ungodly and drunken portion of the community appeared to have been left to themselves, and to commit sin with greater boldness and presumption. The Christian Church seemed too feeble to make direct efforts to withstand these increasing evils.

"But, through the goodness of God, the state of our neighbourhood is completely changed. Many of the young people who had sold their religious birthright, and had gone astray through the influence of sin and the world, are now arrested, and brought back again into the Church of Christ. Many prodigals have been reclaimed, and with humble contrition have sought and found their Father's house. Rioting and drunkenness are rapidly decreasing, the public-houses are emptied, the noisy mirth usually proceeding from such places is no longer heard, the coarse oaths and profane expressions are abandoned and hated, the most presumptuous are now afraid of sinning openly—the sermons heard, and the advice received long since, are now remembered by very many, and seem to come with fresh power, so as to awaken the conscience, and to fill the soul with anxious concern. This takes place at midnight in bed, on the roads, or when busily engaged at their work in the midst of the rocks. Thus God is saving the souls of men from sin and wrath! Life has been breathed into the dry bones, and already there is 'an exceeding great army' of quickened souls in this populous place and the surrounding district.

" Party spirit and sectarian contentions have disappeared —the narrowness and prejudice with which Christians of various denominations regarded each other are fast dying away—and instead of these things, we have instances of love, liberality, and brotherly kindness, reminding us of many of the blessed admonitions given by our Lord to His disciples in His sermon on the mount.

" The spirit of prayer has been given us in a greater degree than ever; this is felt more or less by all who are under the influence of this revival. The people *delight* in prayer, and hence we hear of prayer in all sorts of places, and at all hours. There are not many families in which an altar has not been erected, on which the morning and evening sacrifice are offered. The *gift* of prayer also is given in a marvellous degree : those who can hardly speak at all on other subjects are eloquent before the throne of grace. The old hymns are more appreciated than ever, and some of the anthems and tunes recently introduced are put aside for the present, in order to give place to such as can be used by the whole congregation.

" The Bible also is valued in these days by very many

who took no delight in it heretofore : its pages are anointed by the tears of many Maries and Marthas; its simple verses are as 'the refiner's fire, and the fuller's soap,' purifying and cleansing the unbelieving and worldly heart. It may be said that the Bible-marks of a spiritual change may be found in large numbers of those who have been the subjects of the present awakening—namely, humility, meekness, patience, watchfulness, reverence, and godly fear."—*November* 1859.

Ysgoldy, Llanddeiniolen.—"The public-houses are nearly emptied, and much beer has become useless. We do not now require a police-officer. The influence of religion on the mind will enable every man to take care of himself. The two chapels are become too small tò contain the hearers, and we must shortly enlarge our sanctuaries."—*January* 1860.

Pentre'r dwr, Llangollen.—"This is a small neighbourhood, but proverbial for its drunkenness and immorality. It is now thoroughly changed. The drunkards are made sober, and the majority of the inhabitants are become followers of Jesus Christ. . . . . If this revival should continue, all the people will subscribe with their own hands that they are the Lord's. It is delightful to reflect on the blessed change in the life and general conduct of the people, and especially the young converts. The glory and excellency of the revival is, that 'old things are passed away, and behold all things are new.' Instead of indecent language, oaths, and profanation of the Divine name, while employed in the quarries, the Bible and religion are the chief topics of conversation ; instead of frequenting public-houses, to 'spend their money on that which is not bread,' they resort to the house of God almost every evening in the week, and are seen on their knees imploring pardoning mercy through Jesus Christ ; instead of resembling the beasts that perish, on pay-days and fair-days, they return from Llangollen in good order and in their right minds."— *May* 1859.

Caergeiliog, near Holyhead.—" Religion had been in a depressed state in this place for many years past. The prayer-meeting had nearly ceased to be held, the Sunday school was small, temperance seldom spoken of, a considerable number of people neglected public worship, and were unable to read the Bible. Some of the very worst sins increased, and the great enemy held fast the young people in his slavish chains. But the wheel has at length turned ; he who bound others is now bound himself, and many of his prisoners have made their escape. About two hundred persons have united themselves to the three denominations of this place. It is difficult to imagine the greatness of the change in this neighbourhood. Religion has taken possession of the principal people around us— men who are capable of doing much good."—*February* 1860.

Llangefni, Anglesea.—" Previous to the gracious awakening with which we have been favoured, ungodliness rapidly increased in this town ; the ministry seemed so ineffectual that every messenger of peace, after he had delivered his message, anxiously and almost despondingly inquired, ' Who hath believed our report, and to whom hath the arm of the Lord been revealed ?' Domestic worship was only observed in a small number of families, and the greater number were prayerless. The house of God was wholly neglected by many, and those who attended were cold and formal. The prayer-meeting, notwithstanding the urgent admonitions given, was but small and unpopular.

"But, through the Divine mercy, a change for the better has taken place; multitudes have been 'turned from darkness to light, and from the power of Satan to God.' Blasphemers now pray, Sabbath-breakers remember to keep holy the Lord's-day, drunkards have forsaken the intoxicating cup, and leaving the seat of the scornful, they wait diligently in the courts of the Lord's sanctuary. The family altar is erected in scores of households, and the houses which at one period were the scenes of misery, are now become 'the gates of heaven.'"—*February* 1860.

The following statements have been made in the columns of a Welsh newspaper, by one who had frequent and extensive opportunities of becoming acquainted with the *facts* of the revival in different parts of the principality :—

"1. The additions to the churches amount to many thousands, far greater than has ever been known in Wales within the same period of time.

"2. I have gathered from inquiry that not one person in every fifty of those who have assumed a profession of religion within the last four or six months, has relapsed into the world.

"3. The people generally have been solemnised and brought to think of religious things. I asked an individual near Machynlleth whether the *morals* of the people had improved; he replied, 'Oh, dear, yes, entirely;' and then turned to his wife for confirmation of his statement. 'Yes,' she said, 'they are; every day is a Sunday now.'

"4. A missionary spirit has taken possession of the churches. There is no limit to their desire to save the whole world.

"5. The ministers and preachers are anointed with fresh zeal, and are animated with a new spirit. The churches

and their office-bearers are filled with the ardour of their
'first love.'

"6. There is a great increase of brotherly love amongst
professing Christians, and more cordial co-operation amongst
the various denominations in their efforts to do good, and
to oppose the common enemy.

"These are undoubted facts; and I am sure they have
not been produced by Satan; nor could they be effected by
man without aid from above."—*Glan Alun, October* 1859.

We may add to the above, the testimony of a gentleman
in whose presence the revival was made a subject of jesting
and raillery :—" Say what you please about this revival; I
know this, my servants and workmen serve me better since
it has come amongst us."

CHAPTER VI.

FEW things come in the manner anticipated. The Messiah appeared, but not as the Jews expected Him. Had they read prophecy rightly, they would have seen nothing wrong in the lowliness of His birth, the trials and sorrows of His life, the ignominy and sufferings of His death—all these things had been foretold; but they had pictured to themselves a prince, with distinguished followers, perhaps an armed host, by whose instrumentality he would conquer the Romans, and restore the kingdom to Israel. The kingdom of God, however, came without observation, but not the less powerful and effective because the instrumentality was humble. At the first introduction of Christianity, as in all successive ages, "God has chosen the weak things of the world to confound the things which are mighty, that no flesh should glory in his presence." The treasure has been placed "in earthen vessels, that the excellency of the power may be of God, and not of man." He works by means, and not by miracles, and the means chosen remind us of Gideon and his earthen pitchers, the rams' horns at Jericho, and the stripling David, who proved through God more than a match for the mighty Goliath.

Amongst the principal features of the present revival may be mentioned the absence of great names, its universality, the exercise of prayer, the simplicity of the ministry, the lay element, the aggressive principle, and the outward physical manifestations.

It can hardly be said that this movement has any acknowledged *leaders*—much less can we attach to it the names of men distinguished for learning, eloquence, or eminent pulpit talents. There are such men in the principality, but the revival did not originate with them. The individuals who have been chiefly instrumental in the commencement and spread of the work amongst the various sections of the Christian Church, and throughout the various counties, have been men more distinguished for their piety, zeal, love for God, and compassion for souls, than for high attainments and intellectual powers. This revival has had no Luther or Calvin, Whitefield or Wesley, Rowlands or Harries; and the absence of great names, while at the same time a great and mighty spiritual work has been done, will the more effectually secure the glory to Him who alone giveth the increase.

Nor has this revival been confined to geographical or ecclesiastical limits. It has been seen that its influences have been felt more or less through all the ramifications of the visible Church of Christ, as well as through the various districts of the principality.

God sanctions His own truth. Those who honour the Spirit in their ministrations, and exhibit Christ as the only and all-sufficient Saviour, have prospered in their work. The promise is literally verified—"Whosoever calleth upon the name of the Lord, shall be saved;" whether it be in the church or the chapel, in the dwelling-house or in the barn, the promise is to those who call upon the name of the Lord. Without inquiring, as some have done, whether one mode of worship or ecclesiastical organisation is more favourable than another to the production and development of religious feeling, it is gratifying to be able to state the fact, that at the present time, God the Holy Spirit is at work amongst Episcopalians, Presbyterians, Congregationalists, and Methodists. All who "hold the Head," realise the presence of Him who has engaged to be present where two or three assemble in His name.

Without disparaging the pulpit, or in any way degrading the offices instituted by Christ in His Church, it must strike all, that *prayer*, oral, united prayer, has been greatly honoured of God, as a means of commencing and extending the present movement. The exact *place* of prayer in the great machinery of moral means has been better understood, and the belief in its efficacy has been more fully acted upon now than at any former time.

A correspondent says :—" We expected that the great outpouring of the Spirit would come by means of preaching. It was so in former days—it may be so again—and is so now, to some extent. Thank God, the ministry has not lost its power ; but still, it is quite clear that the Holy Spirit's influence, at the present time, is communicated by means of prayer. Having heard from the pulpit of the ' unsearchable riches of Christ,' we desire to receive them, and this has led us to our knees, to seek and to enjoy. What a traffic there is between heaven and earth ; prayers ascend, and the blessings descend in great abundance !"

Another correspondent, near Bangor, says :—" In several of the chapels prayer-meetings are held at five o'clock in the morning, and again in the quarries during the dinner hour, besides the meeting for prayer held every night. It is as if the whole day and the whole week were one uninterrupted Sabbath. It would be almost impossible for men in the present state to enjoy more communion with God. The house of clay can hardly stand more. I know many young persons and others who have spent whole nights in prayer, in the out-houses, barns, and woods, even when the cold weather has set in. They seem to forget that they are in the flesh."

"I am persuaded that the means blessed of God to create and carry on the revival in *most* places, if not in ALL, is PRAYER. You can trace its origin and progress, in every locality, to prayer, especially the prayers of the new converts, after they have commenced their career. The broken sentences coming from the hearts of those under conviction, and the simple, childlike prayers of young believers, tell most powerfully on all present. Be they converted or unconverted, they cannot help being moved to tears; to the former they are tears of joy, to the latter they are tears produced by a sense of danger."—*Rev. D. Edwards.*

"I cannot say that any indications of a revival could be observed *here* previous to the very day on which it took place. Our denomination throughout South Wales devoted, however, the first Sabbath of last August to pray for the outpouring of the Holy Spirit. *There was no preaching.* PRAYER ONLY. I believe there has been more praying for this great blessing ever since. At all events, the Lord is now doing great things by means of prayer-meeting."—*Rev. E. Jones, Crug-y-bar.*

"Prayer-meetings have been, however, the principal means with us of awakening the churches. In many places union prayer-meetings have been very useful in drawing the public mind toward the great question of salvation. I have been endeavouring for some time to induce all the congregation, the irreligious as well as the religious portion, to attend the prayer-meetings. In order to this, we have held a prayer-meeting for many weeks past, immediately before the Sabbath evening service, commencing at half-past five o'clock. By this arrangement we have succeeded in having all the congregation some time to attend the prayer-meetings, and great good has been the result. Prayer-meetings have been held on the Sabbath, sometimes without preaching, and have been highly useful, when the people were in some measure prepared for them. In most places prayer-meetings have been held for weeks together; and in no instance have such means been persevered in, in the right spirit, without a signal proof of the Divine approbation. But to keep up the interest of the people in such protracted meetings, much depends on their conductors—they must be full of the spirit of prayer themselves. Prayer, faith in God's word, singleness of purpose, earnestness, and perseverance never fail of their object at a throne of grace ; God may be nearer to us than we sometimes dare believe."—*Rev. W. Evans, Aberayron.*

When the public ministry has been the means of conversion in the present movement, it has been of that character which the Holy Spirit ever delights to honour with success—the simple exhibition of gospel truths, poured forth from a heart full of love to Christ.

The revival has come just in time to arrest a growing tendency in some quarters to substitute the wisdom of man for the grace of God, the philosophy of the schools, for the cross of Christ, well-prepared essays and elaborate compositions, for the good, old-fashioned, preaching of Christ and His cross. In the revival districts, at least, the character of pulpit ministrations has greatly altered for the better. A careful observer states :—"This revival has made a great change in the style of preaching, and in the spirit of the preacher. It would appear that the object is,

more than ever, to preach the substantial truths of the
gospel, so earnestly, closely, and personally, that the hearers
may feel that the preacher's aim is to save their souls, and
that God, by *his* means, desires to bring them to Himself.
The people are compelled to believe this. The preacher
comes near them. They feel that he is not within a circle,
and they outside ; they are brought together into close con-
tact. It is not a fight at arm's length, but the preacher
advances immediately to the people, lays hold of them, and
they feel that the sermon has entered into them, and that
the preacher has taken possession of the throne of their
hearts in the name of Jesus. The awakened minister is as
much engaged in seeking to save souls out of the pulpit
as in it. He exhorts, he presses the truth upon them, and
prays with them. Thus he commends himself to every
man's conscience in the sight of God."—*Rev. T. Edwards.*

The *lay element* has been, and continues to be, a prominent feature in the Welsh revival. We do not refer to
that useful class of workers in Christ's vineyard, called lay-
preachers, but to Christian men and women generally.
Whatever may have been the number of conversions through
the direct instrumentality of the pulpit, it is quite clear
that a vast number have been led to renounce sin, and to
lead a religious life, by the agency of those who had no
other qualification to do good to others than their knowledge and experience of the value of religion in their own
souls. Parents have been instrumental in the conversion
of their children, and, in many instances, children have been
the honoured instruments of leading their own parents to
seek a Saviour. Husbands and wives have been made
useful to each other. God has honoured with His blessing
the well-meant though imperfect efforts of humble Christians, who have sought to benefit their fellow-creatures.

Never was there a better illustration of the value and efficacy of individual effort to spread the truth than that which is furnished in every revival locality—no one, for aught we know, suspects that this is morally wrong,—it cannot be said to be unscriptural, for " The Spirit and the bride say, Come. And let him that heareth say, Come. And let him that is athirst come. And whosoever will, let him take the water of life freely." (Rev. xxii. 17.)

There is a principle inherent in Christianity which is embodied in efforts to do good to others. And in connexion with this revival, the converts, as soon as they get good themselves, are anxious *to do good to others*. This is the *aggressive* principle. The commission formerly was, " Go ye into all the world ;" it is the command still, and it cannot be said that efforts to do good should be confined to one class or order of persons, much less that labours for the salvation of sinners should be confined by strict geographical boundaries. In numberless instances since the commencement of this religious movement, have we found the utmost readiness on the part of the converts to *go* anywhere, and to *do* any kind of service, if by any means they might spread the name of their Saviour, and bring souls to Him. Without any regular authorisation, many have gone forth amongst their neighbours to speak of Christ, and to warn sinners to " flee from the wrath to come." Thus, Sunday schools are originated, prayer-meetings established, and the ground prepared for the more regular and public ministrations of the sanctuary. A few instances may now be given with a view to shew that, while the revival spirit leads ministers and people to the adoption of new and untried means, they are greatly encouraged by the evident blessing which attends their labours. The students of at least three of the Welsh colleges have gone forth, not only to the nearest localities, but occasionally to considerable distances, with a view to attack the enemy in his own stronghold. Meetings for prayer have been held in taverns and public-houses; and wherever a district or village is thought to be more than ordinarily indifferent to the claims of religion, young people and others go to such places, and get permission to introduce religious services.

A friend at Denbigh says:—"This revival assumes a missionary character. A number of persons turn out on the right and on the left to hold meetings for prayer, and that, not only in various districts of the town, but also in the surrounding country; and those visits are truly blessed and profitable."

The Rev. B. Williams, of Dowlais, communicates the following facts:—"The idea of holding a prayer-meeting at Morlais Castle on Sunday morning struck these youths.

"Morlais Castle is a place where, on fine Sunday mornings, scores of the worst characters [from the iron-works] meet to drink and fight. They buy the beer on Saturday night, and carry it up there about four o'clock on Sunday morning. There is no house near; they cannot therefore get the drink in any other way. You may imagine what a den of wickedness that place is on Sunday morning. On a fine Sunday morning in June last, about twenty young lads could be seen wending their way thither, and they reached the polluted spot about half-past five. There were scores of the characters mentioned in the place before them, who had already commenced their evil doings. One young lad said to them, that they had come to hold a prayer-meeting, at which idea the drunkards scoffed. But at such a welcome they were not discouraged. A Testament was opened and a part of a chapter read; a hymn was sung, and most melodious it was in the breeze of the morning.

By this time all had become quite serious. Not a laugh or a jest passed—nothing was heard but prayer and praise. Many a rough face was bathed with tears. When the meeting closed, every one went home. All was serious and quiet. The beer was thrown away. Many swore emphatically that they would never go to Morlais Castle again for such a purpose. Many of them are known to have kept their word. This was continued for several Sabbath mornings, and in less than a month hundreds met on the highest summit of Morlais Castle to worship their Creator. This fact needs no comment. We must wait till the day of judgment to know what amount of good was done through this simple instrumentality. These young lads would, after the evening service at the chapel, meet in the woods, and by themselves hold a prayer-meeting, and at ten o'clock at night the hills and woods would echo the praises of God, and the effect was most thrilling. In calling these things to mind, I can hardly restrain my feelings."

The Rev. Gwesyn Jones, of Merthyr, states :—" Out-door services proved a great blessing here. We have had as many as three services on Sunday afternoon, and three on Friday evening in different parts of the town, every one of which was attended by hundreds. Many have joined the church at Bethesda who had never attended any place of worship before they heard these out-door sermons. One young man sold his dancing-shoes and boxing-gloves and bought a New Testament, and in a short time became a member with us, and appears now a very promising character. Of course, it is too soon to speak very positively of men who have thus suddenly been brought out of darkness into marvellous light. Whatever they may prove hereafter, the change effected in them is far beyond human power to effect."

But it will probably be asked, What are the outward MANIFESTATIONS of the revival in Wales? It would be easy to answer this question if it could be said that in all places, and at all times, they were uniformly the same. Like other great religious movements, it must be seen to be understood, and felt to be described. There are no physical prostrations of such severity as to deprive of sense and motion for the time. I am not aware that men, women, and children are "*struck*," as in Ireland ; but multitudes, of all ages are so pierced to the heart by convictions as to produce emotions strong and deep and overpowering. The Welsh revival is characterised by solemnity of feeling and seriousness of manner. This was especially the case at the commencement. There were exceptions then, and there are many more exceptions now. There is loud weeping, as well as subdued sobbing. We may hear the groanings of the prisoners, and the sighings of such as are contrite. For hours together we might witness what may be called "strong cries" for mercy, accompanied by floods of "tears." In many cases, there is rejoicing of soul, expressed in impassioned singing, and long-continued, and oft-repeated hallelujahs of praise to "Him who loved us, and gave Himself for us."

All this may appear absurd, foolish, fanatical ; the sanctuaries of worship may present, on some occasions, scenes resembling those of Babel, and even serious Christians, who desire to "do all things decently and in order," may feel shocked by these apparent irregularities. I am not concerned to defend what I cannot fully explain, but, after all I have seen of the present and of former revivals, I am inclined to say, "Let these men alone ;" let the wind blow where it will ; let the advancing tide fill all the creeks and channels to which it may find access. There are great and

mighty truths in the Bible, which possess a moral force
sufficient to alarm any conscience, and to shake the
strongest nerves. There are joys in religion sufficiently
elevating to inspire feelings of ecstatic and inexpressible
delight—even "joy unspeakable and full of glory." Scripture abounds with examples. It will probably be said
that the Welsh and the Irish are an excitable people.
Granted; but are they the *only* people who are moved in
the presence of great truths, whether of terror or of joy?
It is said that a gentleman of strong nerves fainted and fell
when he heard of the destruction of the *Royal Charter*.
And why? It was because his wife and children, with all
his property, were on board! He saw at once that he was
bereaved, impoverished, ruined; and hence his strong emotions. The man who suddenly wakes up and finds himself
on the brink of a yawning precipice, will not apologise for
the hurried manner in which he starts back to save his life.
The father who, in the darkness of night, finds himself and
his family enveloped in flames, will not be concerned as to
the particular tones in which he shall shout "Fire! fire!"
With much the same indifference as to propriety of tone
and manner, many of the newly awakened seek for mercy,
because they need it, and again praise God for His pardoning grace when they have found it. Great truths which
had been read and heard before without the least concern,
are now become *realities*. The soul is in danger—on the
brink of, almost *in* hell; they see it—they feel it; and in
deep mental distress *cry* for deliverance. A Saviour is
revealed to them in their despair; they behold Him—believe in Him; they are rescued—saved; they know it, they
rejoice, and in forgetfulness of themselves, and indifferent
to all around, they sometimes *leap for joy!*

It should be stated, however, that judicious ministers

and elders do not *encourage* what may be regarded as an excessive exhibition of feeling, more especially when it interferes with the usual order of the public service, or when it disturbs and hinders the devotions of others. They submit to it as an accompaniment, for the time, of a strong religious awakening; they look upon it as the smoke which indicates the kindling of a fire; as the cry of new-born infants—an unmistakeable sign that Zion has become "a joyful mother of children."

CHAPTER VII.

CONCLUDING REMARKS.

ON a very stormy night, when the lightning flashed, and the thunder rolled, the celebrated author of "Night Thoughts" walked into his garden. On his return to his family and friends he observed, "It is a fine night; the Lord is abroad." In the preceding pages, an opportunity has been afforded to "behold the works of the Lord;" not indeed in the desolations of earth, or in the awe-inspiring thunders of heaven, but in the still more wonderful works of His grace. When we see the Church revived, putting on her beautiful garments of holiness, and putting forth the strength of faith, prayer, and renewed energy—when we see these changes wrought in the principles, habits, and lives of such large multitudes, we may well say, in a higher and nobler sense, "THE LORD IS ABROAD." It is said of those who seek pleasure in the things of time and sense, "They regard not the work of the Lord, neither consider the operations of His hands," (Isa. iv. 12;) while, on the contrary, it is the privilege of "the pure in heart" to "see God" in the dispensations of His providence, and the marvellous manifestation of His Spirit's power in the salvation of men.

Revivals, like everything else, will be freely canvassed by the friends and foes of religion; nor should we be surprised to find, that while some are "glad, and rejoice, and give honour to God," there are others who hesitate and doubt, and perhaps a few who dare go so far as to condemn the whole movement. Amongst the objections most frequently brought forward are the following :—It is a man-made revival ; the chief instruments in it are not persons of any weight or character ; women and children are the subjects of it; it is mere excitement and enthusiasm, and although many persons of disreputable conduct seem to be for the present changed, yet, when the excitement ceases, they will return to their former habits, and their end will be worse than their beginning. We are not concerned to answer all these objections. The facts already stated carry with them a power which must disarm prejudice, and disincline even the unsympathising spectator to judge anything before the time. If it be the work of man, how great then must be his power ! By all means let him exert it—let him exert it always, and in all places ! The weakness of the instrument is no argument against the reality of the work. Had it pleased the great Sovereign of His Church to choose the learned, the intellectual, the eloquent, to take the lead in this revival, the temptation would be still greater to say, "This is the work of man." Those who are best acquainted with the work, especially as it bears upon the personal character of multitudes, are the most ready to acknowledge —" A greater than man is here !" And, surely, it can be no objection to the movement, to find that a large number of women and children are brought under its influence. Should we not rather rejoice in this very circumstance, that, as of old, the most devoted, loving, persevering followers of Christ, should be found amongst the gentler sex ; and that even now, *children* are found crying, " Hosannah to the Son of David !" But, it will be said, the *noise*—the *con-fusion*—the loud and long prayers—and singing, with various excesses of feeling, and extravagance of language, —these are most offensive! It may be so, but it may be asked, whether *life* in any form is not better than death, and the dull uniformity of the gravestones? Besides, these things will not last; let us bear with them for a while—check everything that is positively wrong—encourage and strengthen all that is morally right.

There are prophets of evil:—The "converts," it is said, will ere long be "perverts." They will go back, betray religion, and bring disgrace on the whole movement! Suppose this should be found true in part, where would be the marvel? Is not the kingdom of heaven compared to ten virgins, of whom five were foolish? and to a net cast into the sea, which gathered of every kind? And is not the Christian Church a field in which wheat and tares grow together until harvest? We must be prepared for disappointments—a Judas will appear here—a Demas there—Simon the sorcerer, Diotrephes, and men of kindred spirit, will "arise" again. It has been so after former revivals, and we have no right to expect that the present will be an exception. Thus far, however, the great majority remain steadfast—"adorning the doctrine of God our Saviour in all things."

What an amount of responsibility now rests upon the ministers of religion of every name! With greater emphasis than ever are they addressed by the great Shepherd, "Feed my sheep—feed my lambs." It will doubtless be their anxious care to adapt their public ministrations, and social and religious intercourse, to the peculiar necessities of the case. The thousands of additional members may be regarded as children, and as such need to be taught—as recruits, who require to be trained—as newly engaged servants, who must be directed in their work. More than ever does it devolve upon all who bear office in the Christian Church, and all who are qualified by mature experience, to "warn them that are unruly, comfort the feeble-minded, support the weak, and to be patient toward all men;" and so to train the young converts, as to provide for the future exigencies of the Church and the world—able ministers of the New Testament at home—and devoted missionaries, who shall go abroad to "preach amongst the Gentiles the unsearchable riches of Christ."

"THY KINGDOM COME."

"FOR THINE IS THE KINGDOM, AND THE POWER, AND THE GLORY, FOR EVER AND EVER. AMEN."

APPENDIX.

I.

The Author's Postscript, after a Tour in Cardiganshire.

SINCE the preceding pages were written, I have paid a Bible Society visit to Cardiganshire—the county in which the awakening commenced; and having public engagements—either sermons or meetings—at forty different places, I had ample opportunities for making inquiries respecting the revival, and its results. My duties led me into the society of clergymen and dissenting ministers of every denomination; and mixing with the rich and the poor, but more frequently with the middle-class people—such as farmers and tradesmen—I had no difficulty in obtaining information. The difficulty was to find time to record the many interesting facts related to me by persons who could vouch for their truth.

I had already prepared a number of questions calculated to elicit the information I desired; such as—

Have you had, or have you now, a revival of religion in this place?

How, and when did it commence?

What additions have been made to the churches in this place and district?

How many of those who were received as candidates have been admitted into full communion ?

Have you had many, or *any* cases of backsliding ? and what were the temptations or occasions which led to it ?

What is the general conduct of the new professors at home, from home, and in their daily occupations ?

What efforts are made to instruct and employ the converts ?

Do you take advantage of the present state of feeling to abolish at once, and for ever, those disgraceful customs which have for ages prevailed, and which have proved so injurious to the morals of young people ?

The replies to these questions, and the conversations to which they gave rise, would fill a volume. A few brief notes will now be given.

1. At the forty places visited, embracing about two-thirds of the entire county, the additions to the churches of various denominations had been about *seven thousand.* Of these, more than six thousand had been actually admitted to the Lord's table. The relapses had been in the proportion of one in twenty. In some places *all* had remained steadfast. It was stated that some had gone back into the world when the first excitement had subsided, and that others had fallen through intemperance ; while a few cases of immorality had occurred. In a church of two hundred and fifty members, one-half of whom had been recently admitted, there had been only one case of discipline ; and when I asked the cause, my informant (himself a recent convert, and not well acquainted with the language of religion) simply replied, " She had the *shoo* given her for telling a falsehood, and very properly too ; for lying is a very wicked thing."

2. In almost every place I found the ministers, elders,

and deacons, deeply sensible of the immense responsibility of their position as office-bearers in the Christian Church. While they rejoice in the great change effected, and in the accession of such large numbers, they feel that the serious business is yet to come. They will have but little difficulty in directing the new-comers while their consciences are tender and their spirits contrite; but their experience of the past, and their knowledge of the devices of Satan, impress their minds with the necessity of adopting at once a system that will secure instruction, guidance, and government. In short, they are fully convinced that pastoral care must be combined with ministerial teaching. It was gratifying to find that in some places Bible-classes had been formed for the instruction of young people on week-day evenings, in addition to the religious advantages of the Sunday school. Well knowing that the statistics of illegitimacy have been a black spot in the otherwise fair moral character of Cardiganshire, I was delighted to find that special efforts were made in many parts of the county with a view of abolishing those customs of the young people which furnish the occasion of sin and sorrow. Meetings have been held, in which special attention has been directed to the subject; an excellent tract has been issued (in Welsh) by the authority and under the sanction of the Calvinistic Methodist Monthly Meeting, or Presbytery, and freely distributed amongst the people. In several places a *society* has been established, with *rules* and *pledges*. Heads of families engage not to allow unseasonable visits to their houses, and young people engage that all their intercourse shall be at proper hours and in suitable places. It is generally felt that this is the proper time to make a vigorous and united attempt to slay the two great giants of intemperance and immorality; and thus, in cleansing the land from pollution, to save the Church from trouble, reproach, and sorrow.

3. It was natural that I should make some inquiry respecting the instruments first employed in this awakening, and the correctness of the statements already published as to its origin and early progress. I found that the main facts were perfectly correct. I had the pleasure of meeting the Rev. David Morgan, of Yspytty, at one of my meetings, and of hearing from his lips in private conversation many interesting facts of individual conversion in different parts of the principality. He is still " strong to labour," and is constantly engaged in the great Master's service, both in and out of his own county. He is, for the present, a general evangelist, with a roving commission, and having the whole of Wales for his parish. He is preserved, thus far, from strange notions, and, it is hoped, from spiritual pride, self-conceit, and vain-glory.

I was sorry to find that Mr Humphrey Jones, who was made so useful at the commencement, had been laid aside from public work. Physical debility, mental depression, and a change of views as to the mode of promoting a revival, were mentioned as the causes of his seclusion and silence. At present he takes no part in the services of the chapel of his own denomination, (the Wesleyan,) though urged to do so. It is said that he spends much time in *private* prayer, and professes to be too much *straitened* to engage in any *public* exercise, whether prayer or preaching ; but still entertains the hope, if he does not fully believe, that he will yet be made useful to his countrymen. It is a comfort to know that the great Head of the Church is not limited in the use of instruments, and that, whatever may be the character of the instrument, " the excellency of the power" *to save* " is of God, and not of men." The revival work has long since passed into other hands, and however Mr Jones may have been instrumental in kindling the flame in a few localities on his first return from America, other ministers and laymen, not a few in number, and connected with other and (in Wales) more numerous sections of the Christian Church, have gone forth and " wrought in the work"—God, by His Holy Spirit, bearing testimony to the word of His grace.

A Wesleyan minister, in a letter recently received, has very properly remarked—" I prefer a revival coming, as it were, spontaneously from the Divine blessing attending the regular means of grace, to that produced by irregular and questionable proceedings. I dread experiments to get up a revival, and anything that tends to supersede the ordinances of God. We should certainly acknowledge the hand of God in the recent revival, as clearly displayed in the effects produced; but we should also mark for our future guidance, and for warning to others, the evils and abuses which have appeared, through the cunning of Satan and the infirmity of human nature."

The evils to which this judicious minister refers are more *local* than general, and arising out of the circumstances to which reference has been made. The opinion generally expressed respecting the revival, and those who profess to have felt its influence, corroborates most fully the views taken, and the statements made by myself and others in these pages.

4. Although the strong emotions felt and manifested under the ministry, and in the various religious services, had given place to a calm and solemn frame of mind in most places, I found there were some few exceptions. The excitement was at its height in some congregations during my sojourn in the county. It was called by some *a second*

awakening, and more powerful than the first. Had it been my sole mission to preach " Christ and Him crucified," it is possible that I might have seen and heard strange things. Even as it was, with the comparatively dry subject of practical piety, manifesting itself in the distribution of God's Holy Word at home and abroad, there were many opportunities of observing the power of truth on the consciences and feelings of the assembled people.

Never shall I forget the scene of indescribable spiritual confusion witnessed at one of the places visited. It was in a large country chapel, and for a week-night, and such unfavourable weather, there was a very large attendance. There were three ministers present besides myself, but I was the only speaker. It was a Bible Society address, mixed with gospel truth, and ending with a close personal application. For some time before the conclusion, emotions strong and deep were felt, and occasionally manifested. Efforts were made to repress the feelings, but during the last prayer, and more especially during the singing of the hymn, the stifled emotions found vent, the sluices were raised, and the strong current flowed! I sat in the pulpit for half an hour to observe and listen; another half hour was spent at the communion-table below; the tide was still rising, and some of the heaviest vessels were now fairly afloat on an ocean of heartfelt emotions. To give an adequate description of the scene is impossible. And yet how delightful it would be to remember the hymns sung, the petitions offered, and the remarks made! The hymns seemed to possess unusual unction, the prayers were more than lip-utterances, and the observations made by parties unused to speak and to teach, possessed power, point, and pathos, not unworthy of Baxter, Owen, and Howe! It was an affecting sight, when strong men sank in their pews and on the floor, and pulling their hair, uttered cries of soul-distress; when young women, no longer able to sit or stand, first bowed on their knees, and then prostrated themselves on the ground; when from the gallery, as well as from the pews and benches below, the voice of prayer and praise, of grief and joy, commingled in every variety of tone, and every degree of loudness! It is no discredit to the heads or hearts of the ministers present to say that they also were overpowered. Had they lost their reason, or the power of resistance? Was it not a fair opportunity to "try the spirits," and to discriminate between the sympathies of nature and the influence of Divine grace? The truth is, there was neither time nor inclination for criticism, much less for censure. "Dust and ashes," and not the judgment-seat, would have been the place chosen during that awfully solemn hour! If any questions at all were asked or thought of, they were—Is this a repetition of Pentecost? Is it the accomplishment of that which is written in the book of the prophet Joel? Are these people so changed in heart that they cannot help shewing it in their life? Will they go home to pray in secret and in their families? And will they give evidence of the truth of their religion by hating sin, loving the Saviour, " denying ungodliness and worldly lusts, living soberly, righteously, and godly, in this present world?" Oh! if they are enabled to do all this, I am satisfied the work is God's. Therefore, "let us be glad and rejoice, and give honour to Him; for the marriage of the Lamb is come, and His wife hath made herself ready."

II.

Letter from the Rev. DAVID CHARLES, B.A., *Principal of Trevecca College, Brecknockshire.**

" TREVECCA COLLEGE,
March 16, 1860.

" MY DEAR FRIEND,—In compliance with your request that I would furnish you with some details respecting the revival in this part of the country, I rejoice in being able to convey to you the pleasing intelligence that our merciful Lord has not left His waiting people in this county without tokens of His favour, by a gracious visitation from Himself, and the attendant blessing. The accounts of the progress of the great work in other parts proved a stimulus to our churches also, and they were led earnestly to appeal to the throne of grace for a similar blessing. The result has been a large accession of members to nearly all the churches of this county. In fact, the number of members in some instances has been doubled, and even trebled. Weak churches have become strong, and many of those which previously had been rather in a desponding state, have been enabled to rejoice in the Lord ; thus verifying, in a sense, the prophetic word, 'A little one shall become a thousand, and a small one a strong nation.' From our observation of the great change that has taken place in several districts of our neighbourhood, we are forced to the exclamation— 'What hath God wrought !'

" Our congregations had been in a very listless mood for many years, and we had all at times felt somewhat discouraged at the small results of our labours for the salvation of souls; and frequently had we anxiously asked—

* This letter arrived too late to be embodied in the work.

' How long, Lord ? Wilt Thou hide Thyself for ever ? Lord, where are Thy former loving-kindnesses ? ' &c. Still we had not altogether despaired, but looked forward in hope, that ' the time, yea, the set time to favour Zion,' would speedily arrive—nor in vain. God never disappoints His waiting people. The ' set time ' has arrived. The Lord ' hath arisen, and had mercy ' upon us, when we were utterly undeserving of it. Let us then, my dear friend, rejoice and be thankful.

" There was, I believe, an impression on the minds of many, some two or three years ago, that God would speedily visit His people. I was myself so impressed. In a sermon preached in the year 1855, the following expressions occur :—' There are signs which cause us to look for the breaking of the dawn again upon the cause of God amongst us. The watchmen of Zion are shewing symptoms of awakening. The ministry exhibits more life and earnestness than in times past, and I believe there is more praying. The breeze of the morning is already blowing, and we may expect the sun to rise before long,' &c. Under these impressions it was, that an appeal was made to the churches to have recourse to the throne of grace—to continue instant and earnest in prayer, *believing* prayer, for the promised blessing. An unusual spirit of prayer has subsequently fallen upon our congregations. People have met together in multitudes, and have been unable to separate ; sometimes spending some six or eight hours together in prayer and singing ; at other times employing the whole night, even to the dawn, in earnest wrestlings with God, interchanged with hymns of praise. It has happened at times that the minister has been interrupted in his public invocations, by the outpourings of one or two full hearts in earnest supplications for mercy. The union prayer-meetings are greatly blessed. It is astonishing to witness the multitudes that crowd to them. Our places of worship are *full* on such occasions, and there are evident signs of deep impressions being left upon the minds of all present. You well know that the Welsh pulpit is famed for the power of its oratory; and truly we have been favoured with shining lights as preachers of the word—men who could wield with Demosthenean power 'the sword of the Spirit,' and sway the listening multitudes that thronged to be captivated by their eloquence. It was no matter of wonder that such men should command the attentive thousands by the magic of their power, when denouncing the ungodly, thundering the judgments of Heaven, or pouring forth the accents of love and mercy to their enraptured audiences. But I am bold to say that the union meetings for prayer drawn together at the present time, equal the throngs to hear our most eloquent preachers. This is a good sign—something must come of it. Is it not already a verification of that promise—'I will pour upon the house of David, and upon the inhabitants of Jerusalem, the Spirit of grace and of supplications?' I have been endeavouring to watch and consider attentively the influence that is abroad in its various phases; and, after very cautious consideration, I cannot account for it except upon the ground that it must be a *Divine influence.* It would appear to descend upon the minds of a whole community at the same time. First of all, there is a certain seriousness; then a larger attendance at places of public worship; then a spirit of prayer prevails. Afterwards it becomes a subject for general conversation; the impressions from divine things and the eternal world gain strength; a general excitement pervades the neighbourhood; and numbers seek for admission into the churches of all denominations, under evident concern for the welfare of their immortal souls. The result of all this is the experience of intense joy and happiness in the minds of all believers; so that if there is joy in heaven, there is a corresponding joy on earth too. I am informed of one locality in this county, that within the district there exists not a single individual to support the kingdom of darkness. All have ranged themselves among the followers of the Lamb! Permit me also to allude to an interesting circumstance that took place in another locality. After the service one Sabbath evening, the church was requested to remain a while. The minister, however, (who happened to be a stranger,) saw no person leaving out of all the congregation, but all remaining seated. Soon he perceived the exchange of smiles among the brethren present, and the manifestation of other symptoms of joy. He naturally asked them the reason of this, when he was answered somewhat as follows:—' We are rejoicing,' said they, ' from the circumstance that, whereas there was only a single person in our neighbourhood who had not become a disciple of the Lord Jesus, he has this evening remained amongst us, and the Prince of darkness has not another in this district to own his authority, and to support his kingdom.' In reference to the union prayer-meetings, I may mention that all denominations unite in them—not excepting, in some places, the rector or vicar of the parish and his flock. There is an excellent clergyman at M—— C——, in this county, labouring in a mountainous district, but doing much good. He unites with his brethren of other denominations in the true spirit of Christianity, and his church frequently presents the sight of a full congregation, consisting of dissenters of all denominations, together with members of the Establishment, commingling their extempore prayers together in turns at the throne of grace, and uniting in earnest supplications to Him who is no respecter of persons. This is an example worthy to be followed. While I would discard many things which I consider as weaknesses and errors, arising from ignorance and a defective education, I yet must say that sufficient evidences exist to convince me that God is surely amongst us, working mightily and savingly upon the minds of multitudes by the powerful influences of His Spirit. Men are convinced of sin, and are 'pricked in their hearts;' and the consequence is, that a change takes place in their feelings, dispositions, and conduct; and with all this, there is great concern what to do to be saved. So far do I recognise the work of God. We must, however, allow that much feeling and strong impressions are induced by *sympathy*. We all know what it is to be affected by another's feelings with correspondent feelings in ourselves. This principle of sympathy acts very powerfully upon us in common life, and we must not wonder if it should be brought into action by the deep solemnity of a congregation, when many eyes are suffused with tears, and many countenances betray great anxiety; while many hearts beat in unison to the soul-stirring message of the gospel of peace. Conviction, however, may, and often does, follow sympathy; and this, again, leads ultimately to true conversion. God thus makes use of a principle in our nature to work out a moral change in the soul of a sinner, as well as to advance the sanctification of the believer. Certainly sympathy is not religion, but religion may not exclude sympathy; and, indeed, it may be the means by the exercise of which the Spirit of God may accomplish His own work of grace.

How great is the privilege of being permitted to co-operate with God in carrying forward His great work; to be fellow-workers with the Holy Ghost in training up

immortal souls for the glories of the kingdom of heaven !
How great an honour is it, also, that the Spirit of God
should condescend to visit us once and again, and favour
us with His saving and reviving influences ! The earnest
petitions that have been, and are being, sent up to heaven,
lead us to expect yet greater things ; and we are looking
forward to that general pentecost of the world, (how near
or how remote it may be, we will not venture to say,) when
the 'Spirit shall be poured upon all flesh, and the earth
shall be filled with the Redeemer's glory.' That the God
of revivals may hasten that glorious and happy period, and
attend the volume you intend to publish with a blessing,
is, my dear friend and brother, the prayer of yours very
sincerely,

" DAVID CHARLES."

THE END.